One thing that I'⟨...⟩ is that we
are often taught ⟨...⟩ not taught
how to actually read ⟨...⟩ Mike Bird is a gift to the church in that he
is an experienced biblical scholar who can distill complex matters
into something understandable, even enjoyable. If you want to
grow in your competence of reading Scripture and have a crack-
alackin good time doing it, read this book!

> AIMEE BYRD, author of *Recovering from Biblical
> Manhood and Womanhood* and *Why Can't We Be Friends?*

Before you can talk about what the Bible says on "this" and
"that," it is important to process what the Bible *is*. Bird offers
clarity and insight on big issues of inspiration, canon, and how
to read the Bible wisely—all in a short seven chapters. I wish I
had this book when I was first learning how to study the Bible.

> NIJAY K. GUPTA, professor of New Testament,
> Northern Seminary

In an age where the ordinary Christian no longer knows who
Josephus is, why reading "literally" could end in errors, or how
the Bible was even put together, the struggle to help Christians
understand the basics about the Bible is real. *Finally, a book I can
simply hand to fellow Christians and say, "Read this!"* Bird humor-
ously tackles the most common gaps and misunderstandings
among Christians in a way the average person can understand:
the nature of texts, good interpretation, the role of history, and
how Scripture works within the Christian community. This
would make a great book for a small group or families at home.
Hear Bird now and thank him later.

> DRU JOHNSON, associate professor of biblical
> studies at The King's College, director of
> the Center for Hebraic Thought

Holy Smokes! This sounds like a cliché, but this is absolutely true—this is a book every Christian or person exploring Christianity should (I'd rather say must) read. The reason is that knowing the true Jesus comes from what we read in the Bible. However, there are so many misunderstandings of what the Bible is or isn't that can lead to poor understandings of Jesus and what it means to follow him. I don't say this lightly, but reading what Mike has written in this book helps us have a rebirthing of how we view and understand the Bible. I urge anyone—from non-Christian to mature Christian—to read this book, as you will never view or think of the Bible in the same way again.

DAN KIMBALL, author of *How (Not) To Read The Bible*, on staff at Vintage Faith Church

SEVEN THINGS

I WISH CHRISTIANS KNEW

ABOUT THE
BIBLE

SEVEN THINGS

I WISH CHRISTIANS KNEW

ABOUT THE
BIBLE

MICHAEL F. BIRD

ZONDERVAN REFLECTIVE

Seven Things I Wish Christians Knew about the Bible
Copyright © 2021 by Michael F. Bird

Requests for information should be addressed to:
Zondervan, *3900 Sparks Dr. SE, Grand Rapids, Michigan 49546*

Zondervan titles may be purchased in bulk for educational, business, fundraising, or sales promotional use. For information, please email SpecialMarkets@Zondervan.com.

ISBN 978-0-310-53885-1 (softcover)

ISBN 978-0-310-13033-8 (audio)

ISBN 978-0-310-538868 (ebook)

Cover design: Rick Szuecs
Cover illustration: © Alhovic/Shutterstock
Interior design: Kait Lamphere

Printed in the United States of America

22 23 24 25 26 27 28 29 30 31 /TRM/ 15 14 13 12 11 10 9 8 7 6 5 4

For Naomi,
whose husband has never once made her a coffee,
but who sticks with him anyway

CONTENTS

PREFACE

Seven Things I Wish Every Christian Knew about the Bible is about the Bible for Bible-believers. It is the result of twenty years of wrestling with Scripture, explaining where it came from, how to interpret it, how to engage with its difficult parts, how to love it, and how to obey it. In this book, I want to share with you what I've learned about the Bible (amazing things!) and what I've learned about people who read the Bible (sometimes weird and scary things!). The Bible says a lot of things and people say a lot of things about the Bible. But the "things" that people sometimes say about the Bible are not always true or even helpful. As such, what I want to do in this slender volume is explain how to think about the Bible and how to get the most out of your Bible. I'm doing this because the Bible is an important book; in fact, in my mind, it is the most important book in the world. The Holy Bible is nothing less than God's message to us, so we need to have a solid grasp of what it really is, where it came from, and what we are to do with it. By the end I hope to change the way you think about the Bible, transform the way you handle the Bible, and inspire you to enjoy the Bible like never before.

I wrote *Seven Things I Wish Every Christian Knew about the Bible* because if you're a Christian, then these are things that you really, really, really need to know! I would go so far as to say that if everyone knew these seven things, if pastors preached about them, if adult Sunday school classes and small groups taught them, then we would not have quite so many of the problems with the Bible in our churches as we do today. Now, you could go to seminary to learn about the Bible in more depth, but the reality is that not everyone has that calling or even the time to dedicate years of their life to biblical study. But as one who has been into the ivory tower of biblical scholarship, I've picked up a thing or two which are worth sharing with Christians who treasure the Bible and want to know the Bible better. If biblical scholarship is a bit like a foreign land, then I want to be your tour guide and interpreter. I want to show you how the insights of biblical scholarship can answer some of your questions about the Bible, enhance your experience of the Bible, and sharpen your understanding of the Bible. This journey into the Bible, I hope, will equip and encourage every Christian to talk about the Bible with confidence and credibility, to handle it responsibly, to wrestle with it earnestly, and to obey it faithfully.

For those who want to know something about me, I am a scholar into all things Bible, as well as an Anglican priest and devoted Jesus-follower. I have one foot in the academy and one foot in the church. I won't lie to you, sometimes this straddling can feel a bit like roller-skating on ice. Yes, I know you don't go onto ice with roller skates; that's precisely the point. Sometimes straddling faith and scholarship feels awkward, weird, and hard to balance. But as a Christian, I take the Bible seriously and get into serious debates about the Bible, from the basic to the esoteric.

As a scholar, I specialize in the study of the origins, meaning, interpretation, and application of the Holy Scriptures. I tell my students that I am basically a professional "Bible nerd." My daily life is consumed with trying to understand the Bible and make it understandable to others. I obsess with the Bible the same way some people obsess about football, antiques, celebrity Twitter accounts, or *Star Wars* movies. I handle the Bible as a job, as a spiritual discipline, and as an all-consuming passion. I love the Bible like Canadians love maple syrup and New Zealanders love a good lamb roast. I have a passion for the Bible, and I hope that passion becomes contagious through this book.

As a priest, I'm concerned with biblical literacy in the churches, seeing Christians grow in their faith, learning how the Bible informs their everyday life, and seeing the Bible grow them in their faith. In my church role I'm also concerned with attacks on the truth of the Bible, troubled about distortions of the Bible, and frequently grieved by the tribal divisions and disunity that result from different understandings of the Bible. My prayer is that the whole church would be unified in its devotion to Scripture and—as we Anglicans say—together we would "read, mark, learn, and inwardly digest" its pages. If this book helps people, however diverse and different, to gather together to study God's word, to learn from it as much as from each other, then I'll consider that alone worth the entire enterprise of writing it.

ACKNOWLEDGMENTS

In writing this book, I owe a debt to the four colleges at which I have taught, including the Highland Theological College (Dingwall, Scotland), the Brisbane School of Theology (Brisbane, Australia), Houston Baptist University (Houston, USA), and especially at Ridley College (Melbourne, Australia). My colleagues and students over the years have helped me to refine my thinking on exactly how to teach the Bible in a way that is refreshing, godly, and effective. I owe them all a debt of gratitude. Also, the team at Zondervan deserves my thanks for their patience and wisdom in guiding this book from zany idea to publishable project. Katya Covrett and Jesse Hillman are the wind beneath my wings: usually warm thermals that send me soaring higher into the heavens, though sometimes like a tornado that sends me crashing to the earth in a nosedive of cold reality. But to be fair, they are mostly warm thermals. Props to Chris Beetham, too, for his keen eye in the copyediting. Thanks also to Lynn and Jim Cohick, who hosted me in Denver, Colorado for a week, which turned out to be something of a writing retreat and enabled me to finish this book. My colleague Andy Judd gave the manuscript a good read; he picked up several errors and made many helpful suggestions, which I have incorporated.

I wish to dedicate this book to my wife, Naomi. We are now in our twentieth year of marriage, and I look forward to many more years of fun and happiness with the one woman in the world who both tolerates me and makes my life all the better. Here's to you, babe!

INTRODUCTION

The Bible is a big book, but it is a cracking good read! It is a mixture of history, literature, and theology. It contains a diverse array of genres including ancient Near Eastern creation stories, Bronze Age law codes, historical narratives, Hebrew poetry, wisdom literature, prophecy, Greco-Roman biography, ancient Greek historiography, letters, and an apocalypse. The Bible is not just a book; it is a library of books, many books, describing the origins of the Hebrew people, the person and work of Jesus Christ, and the spread of the Christian church. Yet its central character is God—the God who creates, who legislates, who rescues rebels, who becomes human, and who makes all things new.[1]

What is more, there is no book that has influenced the politics, history, art, literature, music, and culture of Western civilization as much as the Bible. I submit to you that unless you have a sound grasp of the Bible, you cannot understand

---

1. D. A. Carson, *The God Who Is There: Finding Your Place in God's Story* (Grand Rapids: Baker, 2010).

Shakespeare, the art of Michelangelo, American history, the music of Bach and Beethoven, the musical *Hamilton*, or even TV sitcoms like *The Simpsons*. The Bible is echoed in various facets of our culture, including literature, music, entertainment, and politics. The Bible is felt everywhere, even if rarely respected.

Yet the Bible is a controversial book. Recently, in Australia a group calling itself Fairness in Religion in Schools has petitioned a state government to ban all Scripture classes and religious education in schools, even though the classes are voluntary, because the group regards the Bible as a deplorable book. The Bible is deemed contraband by Communist and Islamic governments throughout the world. Evidently, there are many people who do not want the message of the Bible to be known and shared. In some places, the Bible is subversive literature and a powerful threat to the status quo. If you ask me, this is even more reason why we should read it!

Of course, it is one thing to read the Bible, it is quite another thing to understand it, and it is still another thing to use it responsibly! To be honest, the Bible is very hard to understand in places. Not because it is a book of mystery, magic, or mayhem; rather, because it contains a history distant from our own, it was originally written to ancient audiences in particular contexts, and it was written for us but not to us. If we are to grasp the Bible, what it meant to its original audience and what it means for us today, then we must traverse some historical chasms and learn to interpret ancient cultures as much as our own cultures. Understanding the Bible is rewarding, but it entails work—hard work.

In this book I intend to do some of that hard work for you and get you ready to understand the Bible as God's word for you and your church. Along the way, we will avoid stereotypes, trite answers to tough questions, and superficial accounts of interpretive problems. Instead, I want to help you get your hands dirty in the biblical world, immerse your mind in the strange and unfamiliar world of biblical history, and introduce you to the big issues that the Bible throws up for those of us who would strive to understand it.

The first thing I want to explore is the origin of the Bible. Maybe your preferred Bible is an app on your phone, a website, Bible software, or a good, old-fashioned, leather-bound book with all sorts of aids for the reader. Irrespective of how you access your Bible, the Bible you read came from a long process of composition, copying, canonization, and translation, over some three millennia! The Bible has its own biography—its own story, we might say—about how it grew and came to be. Here I will give you a brief introduction on how the Bible went from ancient religious scrolls to the printed book you can hold in your hands. Spoiler alert: the Bible was not invented by the Emperor Constantine in the fourth century.

The second thing is that we will need to wrestle with the two big "I" words, namely, "inspiration" and "inerrancy." Hold your hats for that one—it's a bumpy ride! In theological jargon, "inspiration" is where we explain how the Bible is both a God-given book and a human-written book. How it is God's word in human language. How God imparts, infuses, or *inspires* his words into human authors. By exploring biblical inspiration, we are searching for an account of the Bible's divine origins and the human process of composition. So biblical inspiration is on the to-do list. Then there is "inerrancy" or "infallibility," a hotly debated domain of discussion. If we believe the Bible is true, then how is it true, and to what extent is it true? Can the Bible have any errors of history, cosmology, or geology? Is the Bible only faultless in matters of religion and ethics? Some folks will just roll their eyes at inerrancy as fundamentalist nonsense, and others will tell you that inerrancy is the centre of their theological universe. But I tell you that we need to affirm the Bible's truthfulness and explain the nature and limits of its truthfulness.

For the third thing, it would be remiss of me if we did not tackle the topic of biblical authority. Assuming that the Bible is God's inspired word and is true—subjects worthy of their own explication—exactly how does God's word work in our ordinary lives? Are we free to pick and choose the bits we like as if it were some kind of buffet? Are we to slavishly follow every precept it contains? Or does adhering to the Bible require a mixture of affirmation (obeying its instructions) and appropriation (figuring out how to implement its wisdom in a world far away from its original authors and audiences)? Not everyone thinks the Bible is an authority, but for those of us who do, we still have to figure out how that authority works out in practice. And let me tell you, it is not straightforward! Moving from Canaan to Chicago is not easy.

The fourth thing is that it is important for Christians to grasp the "back-then-ness" of the Bible. Yes, God's word is in many ways timeless: it speaks to people across the ages;

it transcends cultures, languages, and nationalities. That is because God addresses all people with the message of love in Jesus Christ. But, at the same time, we must remember that before the Bible was God's word to us, it was God's word to others: it was God's word to the Hebrews in Canaan, to the Judean exiles in Babylon, to the Christians among the slums of Rome, and to the persecuted churches of Asia Minor. We are tempted to think that the Bible is about us, about our time, and finds its fulfilment in our circumstances. However, while the Bible is always relevant to us, if we are to really understand the Bible, then we must respect the original historical setting in which the books of the Bible were written. Knowing a bit about historical background, whether for the book of Jeremiah or Paul's letter to the Philippians, will give us some of the best clues for how to interpret it in the present. So, we must learn the importance of historical background.

The fifth thing I wish to provide readers with is a basic introduction to interpreting the Bible. If you ask me, the big issue is not whether one takes the Bible "literally" or "symbolically," but whether one chooses to take the Bible seriously at all. If we are indeed serious about the Bible, if we aspire to be someone "who correctly handles the word of truth" (2 Timothy 2:15), then we need to learn how to read it and teach from it responsibly. All Christians need a rudimentary introduction to the basics of hermeneutics— hermeneutics being the science of interpretation. Have your thinking caps on for how to read the Bible without turning into a crackpot with your own cult, charts, and golf cart.

The sixth thing to understand is the key purposes of

Scripture—which, as I will explain, are knowing God, deepening our faith, increasing in love for God and love for others, and resting in the hope that God is for us in Jesus Christ. The Bible equips us to know God better, it fosters faith in God and his Son, it builds up our capacity for love, and it comforts us with the hope that is ours in the gospel of Jesus Christ. The Bible can certainly have all sorts of functions, uses, applications, and blessings, but chief among them are knowledge, faith, love, and hope. If you get that, then you get the Bible.

The seventh and final thing is the relationship of Jesus Christ to the Bible. Christ is the centre of our faith and the centre to which the Bible itself testifies. Unsurprisingly then, we will spend some time talking about how to read the Bible as if Jesus is its centrepiece and goal. What will be clear is that the Holy Bible is a Jesus-magnifying book.

That is what lies ahead of us. Hopefully by the end of it, you will have a more profound grasp of the what, how, who, and why of the Bible.

1

THE BIBLE DIDN'T FALL
OUT OF THE SKY

If you are reading this book, then you probably have a Bible. As I'm sure you are aware, your Bible did not fall out of the sky, accompanied by a chorus of angels, and land in your lap, featuring a pristine leather-bound cover, the words of Jesus in red, complete with introduction, charts, tables, cross-references, and study notes. No, that is obviously not where your Bible came from.

The truth is that your Bible came from a publisher. The publisher printed a particular English translation. That translation was based on the efforts of a group of translators who worked with critical editions of the New Testament in Greek and the Old Testament in Hebrew and Aramaic. These critical editions are publications of the text of the Old and New Testament in their original languages using fonts and paragraphing to make them readable. Note "critical" here means "scholarly"; it is a scholarly effort to establish the Hebrew and Greek texts based on a study of the many manuscripts and sources available. The various critical editions of the Greek and Hebrew texts that have been made since the Renaissance were based on the study of various manuscripts. The manuscripts have been gradually discovered, collected, and compiled over the last two thousand years and are housed in museums, libraries, and private collections all over the world. Photos, microfilms, and digital copies of these manuscripts are stored in places like the Institute for New Testament Textual Research in Münster, Germany, and the Center for the Study of New Testament Manuscripts in Dallas, Texas. Those manuscripts date from the Middle Ages all the way back to the second century AD and were copied by scribes based on even earlier manuscripts, which are actually copies of even earlier manuscripts, which go back to the dissemination of a text from its original recipients, which in turn is based on an original autograph composed by an author ("autograph" means original author's copy). Sound like a long and complicated process? Well, it was, but this is what I will try to explain in this chapter. Hopefully by the end you'll see just how the Bible came to be.

THE STORY OF THE OLD TESTAMENT SCRIPTURES

There's a funny story about a lady who walked into a Jewish charity shop and asked the attendant for a copy of an Old Testament. The attendant, a young Jewish man, smiled and said in reply, "Sure thing, how old?" You see, Jewish folks only have one Testament, and they obviously don't need to call it "old" to differentiate it from the part that is "new" as Christians do.

The Jewish people call their sacred book the **Tanakh**, which is based on the letters TNK and stands for *Torah* (the five books of Moses, the Law, otherwise known as the Pentateuch), the *Nevi'im* (the prophets), and the *Ketuvim* (the writings, which is a collection of poetic and historical books). Jewish authors writing in the Second Temple period, which ran from 530 BC to AD 70, including the authors of the New Testament, could refer to Israel's sacred texts as "Scriptures" (see, e.g., Daniel 9:2; 1 Maccabees 12:21; 2 Maccabees 2:4; 4 Maccabees 18:14; Matthew 21:42; Romans 1:2; 1 Peter 2:6). In rabbinic literature, written in the first to fourth centuries of the Christian era, Jewish sacred writings are also called "the Holy Scriptures" or "the Book of the Covenant" (based on Exodus 24:7; 2 Kings 23:2, 21; 2 Chronicles 34:30–31). In scholarly parlance, the **Old Testament** is usually referred to as the **Hebrew Bible** as a non-Christianized way of designating Israel's sacred literature.

DID YOU KNOW?

- The Leningrad Codex is the oldest complete copy of the Old Testament in the original Hebrew, dated to the eleventh century of the Christian era.
- The oldest copy of a complete Old Testament book is the Great Isaiah Scroll (1QIsa[a]) from Qumran, dated to 350–100 BC.
- The three longest books of the Old Testament are Jeremiah (33,002 words), Genesis (32,046 words), and Psalms (30,147 words).

The origins and rationale for this tripartite structure of Law, Prophets, and Writings are not altogether clear. It is certainly not a chronological order of composition because the books that make up the Prophets and Writings were composed over several centuries, some were edited over time, and their acceptance by Jewish communities was varied. The three-part division is perhaps best regarded as a grouping based on a common literary character: books associated with Moses, prophetic works, and other writings. This division goes back as far as the first century AD, since in the Gospel of Luke the risen Jesus instructed the disciples that "everything must be fulfilled that is written about me in the Law of Moses, the Prophets and the Psalms" (Luke 24:44), which corresponds to the three-part division of Torah, Prophets, and Writings. Even earlier, in the prologue to Ben Sirach, composed around 117 BC, we read: "Many great teachings have been given to us through the Law and the Prophets and the others that followed them, and for these we should praise Israel for instruction and wisdom" (Sirach 1:1).

DIVISIONS WITHIN THE OLD TESTAMENT/HEBREW BIBLE

Law	Prophets	Writings
Genesis	Joshua	Psalms
Exodus	Judges	Proverbs
Leviticus	1–2 Samuel	Job
Numbers	1–2 Kings	Ruth
Deuteronomy	Isaiah	Ecclesiastes
	Jeremiah	Song of Solomon
	Ezekiel	Lamentations
	Book of the Twelve	Daniel
	Prophets	Esther
		Ezra-Nehemiah
		1–2 Chronicles

The Law

The Law/Torah/Pentateuch—let's just call it "**Law**"—
refers to the first five books of the Old Testament. They
comprise a historical narrative about creation (Genesis
1–3), the first human civilizations of the ancient Near East
(Genesis 4–11), the patriarchs and the birth of the Hebrew
people (Genesis 12–50), the exodus of the Hebrews out of
Egypt and their entrance into the land of Canaan (Exodus,
Numbers, Deuteronomy), as well as regulations pertaining
to Israel's worship and way of life under God (Leviticus). It
is a story of God's promises, his deliverance, covenants, and
commandments in relation to the nation of Israel. You can
read Deuteronomy 26:5–10 for a brief synopsis of the overall
storyline.[1]

While the Law contains a unified story focusing on
God's plan to create a people for himself, there is also a
complex diversity across the Law. We find ancient Near
Eastern creation stories akin to other accounts of the formation of the world, historical narratives about nomads
and kings, various legal codes, national covenants, and
even poetry. The vocabulary varies across the corpus,
particularly evident in a comparison of the law codes of
Deuteronomy and Leviticus. Sometimes the accounts lack
cohesion, as if a narrative has been interrupted by an inser-
tion, as seems to be the case with Exodus 20:1–17, the giving of the Ten Commandments, which intrudes upon the
narrative of Exodus 19:1–20:21. We also see duplication,

---

1. William S. Lasor, David A. Hubbard, and Frederic W. Bush, *Old
Testament Survey*, 2nd ed. (Grand Rapids: Eerdmans, 1996), 4.

as if two versions of a story have been found, as is the case with the story of creation (Genesis 1:1–2:4a and 2:4b–24) and commands about unclean foods (Leviticus 11:1–47 and Deuteronomy 14:3–21). Although the Law is universally regarded as the "Book of Moses" (see Joshua 23:6; Ezra 6:18; Nehemiah 8:1; 13:1; Mark 12:26; Acts 13:39) and something that Moses himself wrote (see Exodus 24:4; Deuteronomy 31:22; Mark 12:19; Luke 20:28; John 1:45), it is impossible that Moses actually wrote *all* of the Law. For a start, it is hard to imagine Moses sitting down to write the account of his death and burial in Deuteronomy 34 or, for that matter, the description of himself as the humblest man on earth in Numbers 12:3. There are also clear indications that many of the patriarchal narratives about Abraham and others are told from the vantage point of those who lived in the land of Israel in a much later time. For example, Genesis 14:14 declares that Abraham chased Lot's captors as far as Dan, even though the Israelite tribal area of Dan did not receive its name until after the Danites captured the territory during Israel's conquest of Canaan (see Joshua 19:47; Judges 18:29).[2] What this means is that the Law is the product of an oral tradition—a mixture of cultural memory and folklore among the Hebrews—that was eventually committed to writing. A formative role in composition is attributed to Moses, then there was a period of transmission, growth, and editing of the traditions and texts which was probably completed by a priestly group associated with Ezra just after return from exile.

---

2. Lasor, Hubbard, and Bush, *Old Testament Survey*, 6–9.

The Prophets

In the Christian Bible, the **Prophets** refers to the books that close off the Old Testament, that is, Isaiah to Malachi. However, in the Hebrew Bible, with its own unique ordering of the books, the *former prophets* refers to Joshua, Judges, 1–2 Samuel, and 1–2 Kings, while the *latter prophets* designates Isaiah, Jeremiah, Ezekiel, and the Book of the Twelve (shorter) Prophets. These two categories of prophetic books are quite different. The first category of former prophets features historical narratives about prophetic figures like Samuel and Elijah, while the second category of latter prophets features books that are specifically attributed to prophetic authors themselves. The former prophets provide readers with the background to Israel's early history and a prophetic perspective on Israel's cycle of sin-rebellion-deliverance, the formation and failure of the monarchy, and the division that eventually separated Israel and Judah. What the latter prophets provide is an overview of Israel's covenant-breaking behavior, God's threat of judgment, and God's promise to restore the nation from exile amidst the rise of the nearby empires of Assyria, Babylon, and Persia.

As with the Law, the prophetic messages have often been through a complex chain of custody before finally attaining the literary form we have them in today. The prophet Huldah, on the one hand, delivered her important prophetic word orally, and it seems she never got a book deal (2 Kings 22:14). Jeremiah, on the other hand, delivered some of his messages in written form from the start (Jeremiah 30:2). It would appear that from the eighth century BC, people started to collect and edit the work of certain prophets for the benefit of subsequent generations, often adding historical material for context (e.g., Jeremiah 1:1). So, when you think of who wrote the prophetic literature, you should picture a whole team—prophets, scribes, historians, and editors at various stages of Israel's history.[3]

The Writings

The subset of Old Testament books called the **Writings** constitutes a somewhat diverse and miscellaneous collection of documents. First, it contains *wisdom literature*, writings which claim to discern the providence and purposes of God in human life, including Job, the Psalms, and Proverbs. Second, there are the *scrolls* (called *Megillot* in Hebrew), comprised of the Song of Songs, Ruth, Lamentations, Ecclesiastes, and Esther. Third, there are *histories* in the form of Chronicles, which revisits the history of the Israelite monarchy from the perspective of the other side of exile, and Ezra-Nehemiah, which is concerned with the rebuilding of the temple and various other trials during the postexilic period. Fourth, there is Daniel, a mixture of court tales, prophecy, and symbolic visions relating to God's people during the Babylonian exile, explaining their return to the land under the Persians, and forecasting the Greek conquest of the ancient Near East.

The Old Testament Canon

When it comes to the **Old Testament canon**, the first thing we need to do is define what we mean by "canon." The Greek word *kanōn* and the Latin *canna* signify a

---

3. My thanks to Andrew Judd for this paragraph.

"measuring rod," which means to mark out what is exact or what is straight. In regard to sacred texts, "canon" marks out and defines those texts which are regarded as divinely inspired and authorized for use in the believing community. Whereas *scripture* is an authoritative and sacred book, a *canon* is a sacred and authoritative list of books.[4] Let me add that it is important to remember that a canon *does not make* the books authoritative; rather, it *formally* recognizes what was *informally* intuited by the believing community: that a given book is authoritative because it is perceived to have been given by God and delivered through a human agent. So, for example, Jeremiah's message is God's word whether we choose to bind it in a premium leather book with "Holy Bible" printed on the cover, or whether we choose like Jehoiakim to burn Jeremiah's scroll column by column because we don't like what it says (Jeremiah 36:23).

In some sense, the Christian movement had a canon of Scripture at its very beginning, even prior to the writings of any apostolic texts. Jesus and his earthly followers themselves had a collection of sacred writings. They were all Jews, and they fully accepted the authority of books that came to be included in what later Christians would call the "Old Testament."

—*Bart D. Ehrman*, Lost Christianities: The Battle for Scripture and the Faiths That We Never Knew (*Oxford: Oxford University Press, 2005*), 231–32.

---

4. Bruce M. Metzger, *The Canon of the New Testament: Its Origin, Development, and Significance* (Oxford: Clarendon, 2009), 283.

The process of canonization is complicated because nowhere does any book in the Bible tell you which books should be in the Bible! There is no "Thou shalt regard Genesis to Revelation as canon and spurn those books named 1 Enoch, the Gospel of Peter, and Acts of Andrew" or anything like that. Consequently, different biblical canons developed over the centuries and different canons are still used by various religious communities all over the world.

For example, the **Samaritans**—a small group of them still exists in Palestine to this day—only recognize the Law as authoritative. The **Jews** have the *Tanakh*, which corresponds to the Christian Old Testament. However, when it comes to interpretation of the *Tanakh*, Jewish tradition closely follows the body of teachings contained in the Mishnah and Talmud, a collection of oral traditions based on the teachings of celebrated rabbinic leaders that were eventually written down. **Christians** recognize the Jewish *Tanakh* as canon, but divide it up differently and call it the "Old Testament." They also recognize the twenty-seven books of the New Testament as the fulfilment of the Old Testament.

When it comes to the canonisation of the Tanakh/Old Testament, we do not have all the details, but it seems to have emerged something like this.

First, going by citations of the Tanakh/Old Testament in Jewish and Christian literature of the first centuries BC and AD, the Law of Moses was clearly common to all Jewish groups, and we get the impression that several of the prophetic books and writings were also quite popular. More often than not, scholars tend to regard the Hasmonean period (ca. 140–40 BC), a brief period of Judean independence from foreign domination, as the time when the Hebrew Bible was unofficially codified. That is to say, no council ever officially declared these books to be the "canon," but the books deemed to comprise the collection of Jewish sacred literature were established by common practice and general consensus, even if it was a bit fuzzy around the edges.

Second, proof of this is that the entire Tanakh/Old Testament, except for Esther, appears in the Dead Sea Scrolls, a collection of ancient texts found at Qumran near the Dead Sea, which can be safely dated to prior to AD 70. That said, it needs to be pointed out that the Qumran sectarians who copied and housed the scrolls also felt free to compose their own writings in the form of community rules, biblical commentaries, and apocalyptic works which were also afforded authoritative status. The Qumran scrolls are evidence for the emerging consensus about the books of the Tanakh/Old Testament, but they also suggest that the Jewish canon was far from closed.

Third, the earliest list of books that make up the Tanakh/Old Testament comes from Jewish historian Josephus, writing in the 90s AD.[5] He refers to twenty-two books that were revered by the Jews. These include the five Books of Moses (Genesis, Exodus, Leviticus, Numbers, and Deuteronomy), four books of "hymns" or "rules for

---

5. Josephus, *Contra Apion* 1.37–42.

living" (Psalms, Proverbs, Ecclesiastes, and Song of Songs), then presumably the prophetic books and histories, though without saying precisely which ones. His twenty-two-book list is shorter than the standard twenty-four books of the Tanakh/Old Testament. That might be because he either omitted a couple, like Ruth and Esther, or perhaps conflated Jeremiah and Lamentations, Ezra and Nehemiah, or Ruth and Judges. Around the same time, in the book called 4 Ezra, an apocalyptic work written after 70 AD, we find reference to the "twenty-four books" that make up the Jewish Scriptures.[6]

Fourth, Christians largely inherited the Tanakh/Old Testament from their Jewish heritage as followers of Jesus. However, the church largely preferred the "Septuagint," the name we give to a family of Greek translations of the Old Testament. The Septuagintal texts sometimes differed in wording from the Hebrew texts (quite notably in places like Jeremiah). In addition, many writings from the "Apocrypha" (more on that below), like Tobit and Judith, which do not appear in the Hebrew Bible, do appear in Christian versions of the Old Testament in Greek. It was not until Jerome in the fifth century that Christians strove to bring their Latin Bibles more closely into alignment with the Hebrew text and canon, by translating directly from them, rather than relying on the Septuagint for the Old Testament as had largely been done in the past.

---

6. 4 Ezra 14:45.

WHAT IS THE SEPTUAGINT?

The Septuagint is a very fascinating document and a part of our Christian heritage even as Protestant Christians. The Septuagint is an ancient translation of the Hebrew Bible into Greek. It began to be produced, we think, about two-and-a-half to three centuries before the birth of Christ, in Alexandria, Egypt. The first part of the project was to produce a translation of the Pentateuch. [It] was probably the first major translation from one language into another that ever happened in the world. Then as other books of the Old Testament were translated into Greek, by extension they came to be called the Septuagint as well. Now, the word Septuagint is derived from the Latin word for the numeral 70, septuaginta. The reason for that is the tradition is that the Pentateuch was originally translated by 70 or maybe 72 translators. We have both numbers in the traditional stories of how the translation was produced.

—Karen Jobes, interview with Timothy George, *Beeson Divinity Podcast*, episode 321, January 3, 2017.

WHAT IS THE APOCRYPHA?

The so-called Apocrypha, from the Greek *apokryphos* for "hidden," refers to a number of books written by Jewish authors that were widely read by Jews and Christians, but were regarded as of questionable authorship or having dubious origins. This is why Jews omitted them from their canon and why Christians eventually assigned them secondary status.

While the Apocrypha has been read and studied throughout church history, Christian churches differ among themselves when it comes to the status and extent of the Apocrypha.

On the status and order of these books in the Bible, **Protestants** call these books "Apocrypha" and ordinarily place them between the Old and New Testaments, at least in the Tyndale-Matthews Bible, the Great Bible, the Bishops' Bible, the Geneva Bible, and the King James Bible. Fun fact, the King James Version (KJV) originally included the Old Testament, New Testament, and Apocrypha, and it was not until the 1880s that Bible societies began to omit the Apocrypha from printings of the KJV. Even today, many Bibles, like the English Standard Version and the Common English Bible, include the Apocrypha in some printings. The reading of the Apocrypha was encouraged by Protestant denominations, not because the Apocrypha should be used in preaching or in the establishment of Christian doctrine, but because "they were received to be read for the advancement and furtherance of the knowledge of history and for the instruction of godly manners" (Geneva Bible) and "for instruction in life and manners" (Anglican 39 Articles). In contrast, **Catholics** recognize them as "deuterocanonical," a second canonical collection, not merely useful but God-given and authoritative. The **Greek Orthodox Church** recognizes the Old Testament and Apocrypha, but doesn't divide them up into those two categories, and they simply consider them to be *anagignoskomena*, meaning "books to be read."

VARIED VIEWS ON THE APOCRYPHA

- Negative—According to the Westminster Confession of Faith 1.3 (1647): "The books commonly called Apocrypha, not being of divine inspiration, are not part of the Canon of Scripture; and therefore are of no authority in the Church of God, nor to be any otherwise approved, or made use of, than other human writings."
- Positive—According to the Anglican Catechism of the Anglican Churches of North America (2020):

The fourteen books of the Apocrypha, historically acknowledged by this church, are pre-Christian Jewish writings that provide background for the New Testament and are included in many editions of the Bible. They may be read as examples of the faithful living but "not to establish any doctrine" (quoting from article 3 of the Thirty-Nine Articles of Religion).[7]

To make things ever more confusing, there are disagreements on what books should be in the Apocrypha. Alas, the Protestant *apocrypha*, the Catholic *deuterocanonicals*, and the Greek Orthodox *anagignoskomena* do not all contain the same set of writings. If that were not complicated enough, consider this: the **Slavonic Bible**, a literary forebear of the Russian Synodal Version (the standard Russian Orthodox Bible), has

---

7. J. I. Packer and Joel Scandrett, *To Be a Christian: An Anglican Catechism* (Wheaton, IL: Crossway, 2020), 35.

slight variations from the Greek Orthodox Bible in terms of which apocryphal books it includes. Somewhat more exotic, the **Ethiopian Orthodox Church** includes in its Old Testament the entire Hebrew canon and the Apocrypha, but also adds in "pseudepigraphical writings" (texts falsely or fictitiously attributed to ancient figures) such as *Jubilees*, *1 Enoch*, and *4 Baruch*, while rejecting books like 1 and 2 Maccabees. The Ethiopic New Testament includes the standard twenty-seven books but adds many other books related to church order such as the *Didascalia* and the *Book of the Covenant*, giving them a canon with a massive eighty-one books! So, when someone talks about *the* biblical canon, you almost have to ask, which one?

APOCRYPHAL BOOKS IN THEIR MANY CANONS[7]

	Roman Catholic Bible (Vulgate)	Greek Orthodox Bible	Slavonic Bible
The Prayer of Manasseh		•	•
1 Esdras[†]		•	•
2 Esdras	*		
Additions to Esther	•	•	•
Tobit	•	•	•
Judith	•	•	•
1 Maccabees	•	•	•
2 Maccabees	•	•	•
3 Maccabees		•	•
4 Maccabees		*	
Psalm 151		•	•
Wisdom of Solomon	•	•	•

Ecclesiasticus/Sirach	•	•	•
Baruch	•	•	•
Letter of Jeremiah	•	•	•
Additions to Daniel	•	•	•
Susanna	•	•	•

† The books that go under the name "Esdras" are very, very confusing. They can refer to (1) Old Testament Ezra; (2) Old Testament Nehemiah; (3) A combination of Old Testament Ezra and Nehemiah; (4) A Greek paraphrase of 2 Chronicles 35–36 prefacing the whole book of Ezra with Nehemiah 7:73–8:12, plus a tale about Darius's bodyguards (1 Esdras above); and (5) An apocalyptic work extant in Latin (2 Esdras above).

* Appears in the appendix of this Bible.

Let me be clear: Christians should read the Apocrypha! If you want to understand the historical period between Malachi and Matthew, then you should make a concerted effort to read the history, wisdom literature, and apocalyptic hopes contained in this body of writings. The books called by us "apocrypha" were widely read and used by Christians in the early centuries and only gradually were divided away from the Old and New Testaments. The Apocrypha provides a glimpse into the world of Second Temple Judaism and the backdrop to the New Testament period. So *tolle lege*, take up and read!

THE STORY OF THE NEW TESTAMENT SCRIPTURES

The New Testament is the testimony of the apostles to Jesus: who he was, what he did, why he died, how he was raised up from the dead and exalted to the Father's right hand. The New Testament contains a diversity of authors and genres, but if we were to assign a single theme to its contents, it would be this: God is in Christ, reconciling the world to himself. The God of creation, the God of Israel, has made himself known in the person and work of Jesus of Nazareth. And this Jesus, whom the Romans crucified, is Lord and Messiah. He died for our sins and was raised to put us right with God, and salvation is found by putting faith in him.

DID YOU KNOW?

- Codex Vaticanus, dated to the fourth century, is the oldest complete copy of the Greek New Testament. It is viewable online thanks to the Center for the Study of New Testament Manuscripts. http://www.csntm.org/Manuscript/View/GA_03.
- The oldest fragment of the Greek New Testament is the John Rylands Papyrus (P^{52}), dated to AD 125–175, which contains lines from John 18:31–33, 37–38.
- The Gospel of Luke is the longest book of the New Testament (19,482 words).

Gospels and Acts

The first four books of the New Testament are the **Gospels** that tell the story of Jesus's life, death, and resurrection. Matthew is the first Gospel, a book that emphasizes how Jesus fulfils the Old Testament and presents Jesus as the long-hoped-for Son of David. Mark's Gospel is next, shorter than Matthew's, but filled with dramatic panache. Mark underscores how Jesus is the Messiah—not despite the cross, but precisely because of it, the crucified one is Israel's king. The Gospel of Luke is perhaps the most elegant of the Gospels, written in good Greek prose, with a historian's eye for detail. Luke emphasizes the prophetic nature of Jesus's ministry and puts a spotlight on Jesus's concern for the poor and marginalized. Finally, there is the Gospel of John, telling the same story, but with a different texture and with different details in mind. John has long been regarded as the "spiritual gospel," telling the story of Jesus in a distinct spiritual key.

We should not forget the **book of Acts**, the sequel to Luke's Gospel, which traces the beginnings of the church from the day of Pentecost in Jerusalem to Paul's arrival in Rome. Acts is one of our key sources about the early church and the expansion of Christianity into the eastern Mediterranean. It also zeroes in on the apostolic ministries of Peter and Paul and gives us much-needed information about their missionary endeavours. Acts is principally, however, an apologetic work, trying to exonerate the early church from the charge that it was nothing more than a bunch of rabble-rousers who stirred up the Jews and posed a threat to Roman order.

The Gospels derive from a mixture of oral and written traditions stemming from the first generation of eyewitnesses to Jesus. These traditions were compiled by the evangelists into their respective Gospels (see Luke 1:1–4). The Gospel of Mark was probably composed first, around AD 70, according to tradition, in Rome, with John Mark acting as a transcriber of Peter's memoirs of Jesus. Luke and Matthew are usually dated to about AD 80–90. They incorporate most of Mark into their own Gospels, using him as something of a template, but they significantly expand Mark's outline with additional content. They also have their own material that overlaps, like the Sermon on the Mount (Matthew 5–7) and the Sermon on the Plain (Luke 6), either because they shared a common source or perhaps because Luke used Matthew or vice versa. John's Gospel is regarded as following Mark in outline but not in content, since John has his own independent tradition, one indebted to the mysterious figure called the "Beloved Disciple," whom tradition identifies as the apostle John. John contains a mixture of memory and mystery about Jesus, offering a thicker interpretive edge, more concerned with Jesus's significance than merely recounting the naked facts about him. John is the evangelist who wants us to see in Jesus the very face of Israel's God.

Paul's Letters

Paul was the apostle to Jews and gentiles in the eastern Mediterranean, the former persecutor turned proclaimer, who turned the world upside down by establishing largely non-Jewish house churches across Syria, Asia Minor, and Greece. Paul experienced opposition wherever he went. Evidently, many Jews did not like that he was telling them that all the biblical promises were fulfilled in a crucified man, and many Romans did not like that he was telling them that Jesus and not Caesar was the true Lord of the world. Yet Paul, especially through his letters, shaped the church like no other figure of the apostolic era.

There are thirteen **letters** (or **epistles**) attributed to Paul and his coworkers, datable to around AD 48–65, depending on how one correlates the Pauline letters with the book of Acts. Many scholars think that Paul may not have written 1 and 2 Timothy, Titus, 2 Thessalonians, Colossians, and Ephesians because the language and style are different from the other letters that are indisputably Paul's. That is possible; perhaps these letters were written from a Pauline school in the decades shortly after Paul died, something like admiration by imitation. Alternatively, the differences in style can also be explained by Paul using a secretary, the influence of Paul's coworkers, and even just the mood Paul was in when he wrote (remember, the same Shakespeare who wrote the brilliant *Hamlet* also wrote the banal *Titus Andronicus*).

In terms of contents, in these letters we see that Paul was dealing with many controversies in the various churches that either he or others founded. He had to respond to certain immoral behaviors, differences of opinion about how much of the Torah one should obey, financial issues like the collection for the impoverished Jerusalem church, and intruding figures who tried to marginalize him and muscle in on his action. He also advised believers on how to avoid becoming like the pagan world around them. Paul sometimes caught beef with the other apostles, having rather vigorous disagreements with them, mainly over whether gentiles must convert to Judaism in order to be Christian. To that issue Paul gave a definite no: gentiles should not and must not convert to Judaism via circumcision, because that would mean that the Messiah died for nothing (Galatians 2:21). Faith alone is sufficient to save and incorporate gentiles into the church.

Catholic Letters and the Book of Revelation

The **Catholic Letters (or General Epistles)** consist of several writings dealing with pastoral and theological matters. The letter to the Hebrews is a rhetorically rich sermon that basically urges the audience not to go back to Judaism because what they have in Jesus is much better! Although many still think Paul wrote it, the only thing we can be confident about regarding the letter is that Paul did not write it, though perhaps a Pauline sympathizer did. It is often thought to have been composed in Rome in the late 50s or early 60s AD on the eve of the Neronian persecution (though some do date it much later). The letter of James could be the earliest writing of the New Testament. It might have been written as early as the mid-40s AD (James was martyred in AD 62). It was written for Christian synagogues in rural Galilee and Syria, presenting them with various ethical instructions, as well as dealing with a distortion of Paul's teaching on justification by faith alone. Other scholars regard it as a collection of miscellaneous teachings weaved into a sermon, perhaps indebted to James but compiled and disseminated to churches much later. First Peter was written by Peter from Rome to the churches in Asia Minor (i.e., modern Turkey), urging them to contend for the faith under adverse circumstances. The letter of Jude was written by another relative of Jesus and urges the audience to avoid false teachers and to persevere in their most holy faith. Second Peter is essentially a theological tract against heresy with an exhortation not to give up hope for Christ's return. It is very different in style from 1 Peter, incorporates the entire epistle of Jude into chapter 2, has a possible allusion to the Gospel of Matthew, seems to know of a Pauline letter collection that is widely regarded as "Scripture," and the first person to quote it was Origen in the third century. So, most scholars think Peter did not write 2 Peter; instead, it was a kind of "transparent fiction" perhaps attempting to show what Peter would say if he was around today.[8] Scholars date it anywhere from AD 65 to AD 200. The letters of John are addressed to a network of churches around Ephesus at the end of the first century and were written by John the Elder, who was quite possibly the same person as the apostle John (but we can't say with certainty!). In his first letter, John urges believers to follow Jesus's love command and to separate from those who hold to the heresy of docetism (that Jesus did not have a physical body) and to resist those who deny that Jesus was the Messiah (perhaps referring to Jewish Christians who abandoned Christianity and went back to nonmessianic Judaism). In his second letter, John warns the "elect lady and her children," probably a symbolic title for the leadership and laity of a sister church, about deceivers and the antichrist. In his third letter, John writes to Gaius, warning him about Diotrephes and singing the praises of Demetrius.

That brings us finally to the **book of Revelation,** otherwise known as the **Apocalypse of John**. The book is a mixture of a letter, prophecy, and apocalyptic symbolism. John the Seer (not necessarily the same John as John the Elder from the epistles or John the evangelist responsible for

---

8. Richard Bauckham, *Jude, 2 Peter*, Word Biblical Commentary 50 (Waco, TX: Word, 1983), 134.

John's Gospel) had a vision on the island of Patmos about the present, the near future, and the distant future. Revelation contains letters to the seven churches of Asia Minor in modern-day western Turkey (Revelation 1–3), a vision of heavenly worship and Christ's commission to redeem his people (Revelation 4–5), a symbol-laden prophecy of the future that includes the defeat of the Roman Empire and all the enemies of God (Revelation 6:1–19:10), then Christ's return (Revelation 19:11–20:15) and the consummation of the new heavens and new earth (Revelation 21–22). The plot is quite simple: God wins, the Lamb triumphs, and the church reigns with Christ forever!

The New Testament Canon

Much like the canonization of the Old Testament, the people who collected these Christian books copied them, shared them, and used them in worship and preaching. They were convinced that they carried Jesus's words, had apostolic authority, and were in some sense God-given. When some persons made lists about which books were in and out for Christians, they weren't deciding to make certain books Scripture based on their own mood or machinations. More properly, early lists of recommended and rejected books were trying to recognize the authority in the books that were already commanding the obedience of the faithful in the churches across Europe, Africa, and the Middle East.

The consolidation of the **New Testament canon** was a gradual process as the churches came to agree on a definitive list of Christian writings. No one was walking around with an inspiration-o-meter collecting books that measured a high reading. The second-century church held the Jewish Scriptures (usually the Septuagint), the words of Jesus (whether in oral tradition, in the Gospels, or even in other writings), and apostolic instructions (esp. Peter, Paul, and John) in high regard. By the mid-second century, the four Gospels and a Pauline letter collection were widely used and highly regarded. These are the primary writings that were used by the apostolic fathers and early Christian apologists, even if other writings were also utilized by Christian groups.

Athanasius was a bishop of Alexandria, Egypt, in the fourth century, and in his Thirty-Ninth Festal Letter (AD 367), he wrote to his churches about the biblical canon:

There are, then, of the Old Testament, twenty-two books in number; for, as I have heard, it is handed down that this is the number of the letters among the Hebrews; their respective order and names being as follows. The first is Genesis, then Exodus, next Leviticus, after that Numbers, and then Deuteronomy. Following these there is Joshua, the son of Nun, then Judges, then Ruth. And again, after these four books of Kings, the first and second being reckoned as one book, and so likewise the third and fourth as one book. And again, the first and second of the Chronicles are reckoned as one book. Again Ezra, the first and second are similarly one book. After these there is the book of Psalms, then the Proverbs, next Ecclesiastes, and the Song of Songs. Job follows, then the Prophets, the twelve being reckoned as one book. Then Isaiah, one book, then Jeremiah with Baruch, Lamentations, and the epistle, one book; afterwards, Ezekiel and Daniel, each one book. Thus far constitutes the Old Testament. Again it is not tedious to speak of the [books] of the New Testament. These are, the four Gospels, according to Matthew, Mark, Luke, and John. Afterwards, the Acts of the Apostles and Epistles (called Catholic), seven, viz. of James, one; of Peter, two; of John, three; after these, one of Jude. In addition, there are fourteen Epistles of Paul, written in this order. The first, to the Romans; then two to the Corinthians; after these, to the Galatians; next, to the Ephesians; then to the Philippians; then to the Colossians; after these, two to the Thessalonians, and that to the Hebrews; and again, two to Timothy; one to Titus; and lastly, that to Philemon. And besides, the Revelation of John.[9]

Then, by the end of the second century, there arose the need to provide an authoritative list of sacred books for Christian usage due to "heretical" Christian groups either heavily editing apostolic writings or composing their own competing literature (among them were groups such as the Ebionites, Marcionites, Valentinians, and Sethians, each with their own revision of New Testament texts, with varied ideas about Christian faith, and new writings to explain their specific viewpoints). Some early lists of authoritative Christian writings—the Muratorian canon and

---

9. *Nicene and Post-Nicene Fathers*, Second Series, 14 vols., ed. Philip Schaff and Henry Wace (repr., Edinburgh: T&T Clark, 1991), 4:552.

anti-Marcionite prologues—were probably written during this period, and they list the books generally accepted in the churches and thought to have been composed within the circle of the apostles. In the succeeding centuries, several lists of authorized books were put forward, but the books that gained immediate currency included the four Gospels, thirteen or fourteen letters of Paul (Hebrews often included as Pauline), 1 Peter, and 1 John. Generally speaking, Hebrews, James, Jude, 2 Peter, 2 and 3 John, and Revelation were accepted by many churches but still disputed by some.[10] The reasons for disputing them were based on either content (some rejected the millenarianism of Revelation with its vision of a thousand-year reign of Christ on earth) or doubts over their authorship (as in the case with 2 Peter).[11] Several other books also garnered support, such as the Shepherd of Hermas, the Apocalypse of Peter, the Epistle of Barnabas, the Didache, and 1 Clement, but they were eventually rejected by most as either spurious or not written by an apostle.

The criteria for a Christian writing becoming canonical appears to have been:

1. Apostolicity: Was it written by an apostle or an apostolic companion?
2. Antiquity: Can it be dated to the apostolic era?
3. Orthodoxy: Did it comport with the church's teaching?
4. Catholicity: Was it used widely in all the churches?

---

10. Eusebius, *Hist. Eccl.* 3.25.3.
11. Eusebius, *Hist. Eccl.* 2.23.25.

The crystallization of the process of canonization took place in the late fourth century. Athanasius's Thirty-Ninth Festal Letter (AD 367), as well as the councils of Hippo Regius (AD 393) and Carthage (AD 397), listed the twenty-seven books in our current New Testament as canonical.[12]

WHAT ABOUT THE "OTHER" GOSPELS?

It is true that Matthew, Mark, Luke, and John were not the only Gospels written. There was an explosion of Gospels written in the second and third centuries, with the Gospel of Thomas, Gospel of Truth, Gospel of Peter, Gospel of Philip, Gospel of Judas, Gospel of Mary, Gospel of the Egyptians, and many others probably composed during that time. Some of these Gospels may have connections with early oral traditions about Jesus, but more often than not they are derivative of the four canonical Gospels, and their primary value is that they testify to the diverse and varied ways that the story of Jesus was remembered and interpreted by Christian groups who never became part of the mainstream church. Many of these other Gospels are heretical by the later standards of orthodoxy, though not all are, and some are congenial with regular Christian belief. Whereas a few theologians and church leaders saw some value in these other Gospels, they were mostly rejected as being falsified depictions of Jesus—out of sync with the mainstream

---

12. Michael F. Bird, "Canon, Biblical," in *Evangelical Dictionary of Theology*, ed. Daniel Treier and W. A. Elwell, 3rd ed. (Grand Rapids: Baker, 2016), 156–58.

church's faith—and denounced as spurious for teaching things that were elitist and esoteric. They were not rejected because of a conspiracy led by the bishops in cahoots with the emperor to suppress the truth about Jesus. No, these other Gospels were rejected because they set forth a different Jesus, a Jesus different from the Jesus of the gospel of salvation, different from the Jesus of the church's worship, and not the Jesus to whom people were praying. For a case in point, consider the final verse of the Gospel of Thomas (verse 114), which says:

Simon Peter said to them: "Let Mary go away from us, for women are not worthy of life." Jesus said: "Look, I will draw her in so as to make her male, so that she too may become a living male spirit, similar to you." But I say to you: "Every woman who makes herself male will enter the kingdom of heaven." (trans. Stephen Patterson and James Robinson)

A BRIEF HISTORY OF THE ENGLISH BIBLE

During the Middle Ages, the Latin Vulgate was the Bible of the English church. Despite the existence of a few fragments here and there, there was no English translation of the Bible in the common language. But in the 1380s, the Oxford professor **John Wycliffe** began to produce an English translation of the Vulgate. Wycliffe was declared a heretic by the Roman Catholic Church, but his followers, known as Lollards, kept his teachings and translation alive in an underground movement despite English translations being banned by Henry IV in 1401.

Things came to a head when **Erasmus** of Rotterdam published his first edition of a parallel Latin-Greek New Testament in 1516, the *Novum Testamentum*, based on a limited number of medieval Greek manuscripts that he had access to. Not only was this book an original edition of the Greek New Testament, but it was reproduced in large numbers due to the invention of the printing press. Erasmus's *Novum Testamentum* highlighted the disparities between the Greek and Latin versions of the New Testament, which furthered the case for religious reform. Erasmus's *Novum Testamentum* went through five editions over the next twenty years, with each edition attempting to improve the text when new manuscripts were drawn to his attention. The third edition of 1522 served as the basis for **William Tyndale's** illegal and contraband English translation of the New Testament in 1526. A translation of the Old Testament into English was completed by **Myles Coverdale** based on Tyndale's unfinished work, Coverdale's own translation of the Vulgate, and Luther's German Bible in 1535. Thus, it was in 1535 that England finally had a complete copy of the Old and New Testaments in English.

Shortly after, in 1537, John Rogers produced his own translation of the Old and New Testaments in English, largely dependent upon the work of Tyndale and Coverdale, called "The Matthew Bible" because Rogers wrote under the pseudonym Thomas Matthew. Then, in 1539, Archbishop Thomas Cranmer commissioned Coverdale to produce the

"Great Bible," which was the first English Bible officially authorized for use in the Church of England.

Other notable English translations include the Geneva Bible of 1560, produced by the Protestant English exiles who escaped Queen Mary I of England and took refuge in Geneva. As an alternative to the Geneva Bible, there was the Bishops' Bible of 1568. When the Protestant Elizabeth I ascended to the English throne, the Catholic exiles created their own English countertranslation called the Rheims-Douai Bible of 1582 (New Testament) and 1610 (Old Testament). It was, however, the **1611 King James Version** that became the official Bible of the English-speaking world for roughly the next three centuries (though unbeknownst to many, even the King James Bible has had its edits over the years!).

Despite its dominance, the elegant and esteemed King James Version (KJV) began to fade from usage in the twentieth century for two reasons.

First, the textual basis of the KJV eventually came to be outdated by new manuscript discoveries and research in the field of textual criticism (textual criticism is the study of the original manuscripts which our English Bibles are based on).

The New Testament of the KJV was based on a translation of the Greek New Testament text compiled by Theodore Beza (1598), which was based on the edition of Stephanus (1551), which was based on the third edition of Erasmus's *Novum Testamentum* (this is the so-called *Textus Receptus* or "Received Text"). Yet as more manuscripts began to be uncovered by intrepid travelers to the libraries and monasteries of the East during the next three centuries, these manuscripts were used in creating new critical editions of the Greek New Testament, which greatly improved the likelihood of recovering a text closer to the original autographs. Scholars like B. F. Westcott (1825–1901) and F. J. A. Hort (1828–1892) in England, as well as E. Nestle (1851–1913) and K. Aland (1915–1994) in Germany, studied these various manuscripts and refined the methodology for determining from all of the textual evidence available the original text of the New Testament. The new editions were an improvement on the *Textus Receptus* as they were based on older manuscripts and a better methodology for deciding between competing variants. New critical editions of the Greek New Testament have largely provided the textual basis for modern translations like the New International Version, the New Revised Standard Version, the English Standard Version, and the Common English Bible, to name a few.

For the Old Testament, the KJV used the Hebrew Rabbinic Bible of Daniel Blomberg (1524–25), albeit adjusted to fit the Christianizations of the Old Testament found in the Vulgate (Latin Bible) and Septuagint (Greek Old Testament). However, study of the Hebrew text was greatly enhanced by the discovery of the Dead Sea Scrolls in 1946–56 in Qumran in Israel. The scrolls contained Hebrew copies of Old Testament books, commentaries on some of these Old Testament biblical books, and a plethora of quotes and allusions to the Hebrew of the Old Testament. In some cases the scrolls confirmed the relative stability of the transmission of the text of the Old Testament. Copies of the book of Isaiah found at Qumran are more or less identical to the twelfth-century Masoretic Text used to make modern editions of the Hebrew Bible. Alternatively, questions are raised about other books such as Jeremiah, as there are some differences between the manuscripts found at Qumran, the twelfth-century Masoretic text of Jeremiah, and manuscripts containing Jeremiah in Greek. In sum, we now have a greater number of ancient manuscripts to study and a better system for navigating the differences between manuscripts, and we can produce Hebrew and Greek editions of the Bible that are much closer to the original autographs than what scholars could produce in 1611.

Second, the English language has changed since 1611. Nobody—except Shakespearean actors—doth speaketh in Elizabethan English anymore, and even the meaning of English words has changed over time. For example, in 1 Thessalonians 4:15, the KJV reads, "We which are alive and remain unto the coming of the Lord shall not *prevent* them which are asleep." By using the word *prevent,* one might think that Paul negates the possibility that the living can hinder the dead from rising, but that is not the issue at all. The original Greek has the word as *phthanō,* meaning "to come before another," and the KJV committee translated this with the word *prevent*, influenced by the Latin *preveniens*, "to come before another." The problem is that in modern English *prevent* does not mean precede, but something more like "hinder" or "inhibit." This is why modern translations like the NIV are much better—at least as we speak English—by rendering 1 Thessalonians 4:15 as, "We tell you that we who are still alive, who are left until the coming of the Lord, will certainly not *precede* those who have fallen asleep." The KJV was composed to put the word of God in the common tongue, in language that ordinary people could understand, whether a ploughboy working in the fields or a scullery maid working in a mansion. It is because we share that same ethos—giving English-speaking people a translation that they can understand—that we constantly need to revise our English translations to reflect the common tongue.

So that, in a whirlwind tour, is how we got the Old and New Testaments, and how we got our English Bibles.

RECOMMENDED READING

Old Testament

Beckwith, Roger T. *The Old Testament Canon of the New Testament Church and Its Background in Early Judaism*. Eugene, OR: Wipf & Stock, 2008.

Longman III, Tremper, and Raymond B. Dillard. *An Introduction to the Old Testament*. 2nd ed. Grand Rapids: Zondervan, 2009.

Apocrypha

deSilva, David A. *Introducing the Apocrypha: Message, Context, Significance*. Grand Rapids: Baker, 2004.

Harrington, Daniel J. *Invitation to the Apocrypha*. Grand Rapids: Eerdmans, 1999.

New Testament

Burge, Gary M., and Gene L. Green. *The New Testament in Antiquity*. 2nd ed. Grand Rapids: Zondervan, 2020.

Patzia, Arthur G. *The Making of the New Testament: Origin, Collection, Text and Canon*. Downers Grove, IL: InterVarsity Press, 1995.

English Bible

Bobrick, Benson. *The Making of the English Bible*. London: Phoenix, 2003.

Bruce, F. F. *The Books and the Parchments: How We Got Our English Bible*. Old Tappan, NJ: Revell, 1984.

2

THE BIBLE IS DIVINELY GIVEN AND HUMANLY COMPOSED

The Bible is the "word of God," which means that it is a divinely communicated message from God to us. However, as you may have noticed, it is also a very human book. The Bible was written by human authors, in human languages, describing human events, dealing with human issues, and directing humans about all things pertaining to God. So, which bits are divine and which bits are human? Is it possible to differentiate them? Or, we might ask, how did God get his message into, through, and out of human authors? What we are asking about here is traditionally called **inspiration**, which is the explanation of how the Bible can be both from God and from humans. When we investigate biblical inspiration, we are examining the means, however mysterious, by which God communicates his message through human authors like Isaiah, Hosea, Amos, Matthew, Paul, and Luke.

In addition, many theologians claim that if the Bible is inspired—in whatever way—then it must also be **inerrant**, that is, without error. But what does it mean to say that the Bible is "without error"? Is that even true? If so, does it mean that the Bible is true and accurate in every detail, even in historical and scientific aspects? Or does the Bible's truthfulness only extend to the subject of its religious and ethical claims? Theologians have been notoriously divided on what inerrancy means and to what extent it even applies. There has been a whole spate of factional divides over this subject in what feels like a never-ending "battle for the Bible" within evangelical denominations and institutions.

So, in order to explain the divine origins and human texture of the Bible, in this chapter we will investigate the two big theological "I" words: inspiration and inerrancy. It is vital that Christians know *how* the Bible is given to us and *how* the Bible happens to be true. Having a good grasp of inspiration and inerrancy means that we won't treat the Bible like a secret code, unlocked by the symbolism on the back of a ten-dollar bill, nor use it inappropriately as a textbook on adolescent cognitive development, or a reference work on paleontology. We will be free to honor the Bible as it presents itself and to treasure the Bible for the truths to which it speaks. So, hopefully, by the end of this chapter, you'll have a better grasp of just how the Bible is God's word through human authors and be fully convinced that the Bible is truthful and trustworthy in the matters to which it speaks.

DIVINE SPEECH THROUGH
A HUMAN SUBJECT

In canvassing biblical inspiration, we must look at two precise areas. First, the **phenomena** described in Scripture where God's word "comes" to someone; and second, the **plain statements** given in Scripture as to how authors were divinely moved to write Scripture. To that we now turn.

What Inspiration Looks Like When It Happens

There are several examples in the Bible where it is reported that God's word came to a person. Consider the following:

After this, the **word of the** Lord came to Abram in a vision:

"Do not be afraid, Abram.
    I am your shield,
    your very great reward."

But Abram said, "Sovereign Lord, what can you give me since I remain childless and the one who will inherit my estate is Eliezer of Damascus?" And Abram said, "You have given me no children; so a servant in my household will be my heir."

Then the word of the Lord came to him: "This man will not be your heir, but a son who is your own flesh and blood will be your heir." He took him outside and said, "Look up at the sky and count the stars—if indeed you can count them." Then he said to him, "So shall your offspring be." (Genesis 15:1–5)

The words of Jeremiah son of Hilkiah, one of the priests at Anathoth in the territory of Benjamin. The **word of the** Lord came to him in the thirteenth year of the reign of Josiah son of Amon king of Judah, and through the reign of Jehoiakim son of Josiah king of Judah, down to the fifth month of the eleventh year of Zedekiah son of Josiah king of Judah, when the people of Jerusalem went into exile.

The **word of the** Lord came to me, saying,

> "Before I formed you in the womb I knew you,
>   before you were born I set you apart;
>   I appointed you as a prophet to the nations."

"Alas, Sovereign Lord," I said, "I do not know how to speak; I am too young."

But the Lord said to me, "Do not say, 'I am too young.' You must go to everyone I send you to and say whatever I command you. Do not be afraid of them, for I am with you and will rescue you," declares the Lord.

Then the Lord reached out his hand and touched my mouth and said to me, "**I have put my words in your mouth.**" (Jeremiah 1:1–9)

But this **word of God** came to Shemaiah the man of God: "Say to Rehoboam son of Solomon king of Judah, to all Judah and Benjamin, and to the rest of the people, 'This is what the Lord says: Do not go up to fight against your brothers, the Israelites. Go home, every one of you, for this is my doing.'" So they obeyed the word of the Lord and went home again, as the Lord had ordered. (1 Kings 12:22–24)

During the high priesthood of Annas and Caiaphas, the **word of God** came to John son of Zechariah in the wilderness. He went into all the country around the Jordan, preaching a baptism of repentance for the forgiveness of sins. (Luke 3:2–3)

These and other texts envisage a person receiving a "word" from God in the form of a promise (Abram), a piece of instruction (Shemaiah), empowerment to engage in a prophetic ministry of warning and lament (Jeremiah), or a call to proclaim a divine message to everyone who would listen (John the Baptist). They are told something and come away with a profound sense of having encountered the living God. These passages point to a moment of *revelation*, a disclosure of something previously unknown, an event whereby God imparts to a person some kind of knowledge about his purpose and plans, leaving a deeply personal impact upon the recipient: revelation is both *propositional* (imparts knowledge) and *personal* (impacts the person). In other words, they are told something and come away with a profound sense of having encountered the living God.

In several places, the book of Acts describes how a person was "filled with the Holy Spirit" or "full of the Spirit" and then spoke the word of God (see Acts 4:8, 31; 6:10 7:55; 13:9). In addition, in Luke's account of apostolic preaching, there are several references to how the Holy Spirit spoke through Old Testament authors like David in the Psalms or through prophets like Isaiah (Acts 4:25; 28:25). That is in agreement with the Old Testament, where it is frequently claimed that the Spirit spoke "by" or "through" someone (see 2 Samuel 23:2; Nehemiah 9:30; Ezekiel 11:5). Taking these instances together, the Holy Spirit is the main speaker who speaks God's word through chosen persons. God's Spirit animates and empowers someone to speak a message on his behalf.

In the book of Revelation, John's opening description of the revelation that was given to him is called "the word of God and the testimony of Jesus Christ" (Revelation 1:2). This "revelation" includes a mixture of visions, angelic reports, the Spirit's teaching, and even dictation. John urged the readers to "hear what the Spirit says to the churches" (Revelation 2:7, 11, 17, 29; 3:6, 13, 22). In some cases, the Lord explicitly told John to write things down: descriptions of his vision (Revelation 1:11, 19) or else specific words given to him to record (Revelation 2:1, 8, 12, 18; 3:1, 7, 14; 14:13; 19:9; 21:5). John's account of divine revelation includes the reception of amazing visions, a glimpse into heavenly realities, metaphor piled upon metaphor, mysterious intimations of future events, and precise words to exhort the churches of his own day.

When God's word comes to someone, it is riveting, arresting, and frightening because of its power and majesty as well as its directness and gravity. It may be in the form of a vision, but it is not some vague vibe. It may elicit a range of emotions, but it does not consist of unintelligible religious feelings. God's revealed word may sound otherworldly, but it is put into a clear and comprehensible language for its audience. Divine speech has the intimacy of a mother speaking to a toddler and the power of a director showing an actor how to deliver his lines. God speaks a divine word which, through the Spirit, is made intelligible for human consumption, by the wise and the simple alike.

What Scripture Says about Itself

Given that Scripture is frequently described as the "word of God," it would make sense that much of what we have observed about God's word coming upon a prophet would also apply to how the Spirit moved the biblical authors to write Holy Scripture. At this point we will discuss Scripture's own testimony of how it is a sacred word from God and the "mechanism" by which biblical authors were moved to write under the Spirit's influence.

The first key text is from Paul, writing to his junior colleague and protégé, Timothy:

> All Scripture is God-breathed and is useful for teaching, rebuking, correcting and training in righteousness, so that the servant of God may be thoroughly equipped for every good work. (2 Timothy 3:16–17)

What is interesting here is that Paul invents a new word, "God-breathed" (*theopneustos* in Greek), to explain how God communicates a message through the written medium. While we could discuss several possibilities, to cut to the chase, the point is that Scripture is God's word breathed into human authors who in turn compose written texts. This means that Scripture is a product of God's creative and communicative work in human authors, which is so effective that what they wrote under divine influence is considered to be divinely authored. Because of this God-given origin, Scripture is useful for teaching the truth, pointing out error, correcting wrong behavior, and instructing in the disciplines of godliness and holiness.

> Believers receive Scripture as that which is generated by the Spirit to build them up in Christ, to the service of God himself.
> —J. Todd Billings, The Word of God for the People of God (Grand Rapids: Eerdmans, 1996), 92.

Then we have another remarkable statement in 2 Peter about how authors were moved to write a message from God.

Above all, you must understand that no prophecy of Scripture came about by the prophet's own interpretation of things. For prophecy never had its origin in the human will, but prophets, though human, spoke from God as they were carried along by the Holy Spirit. (2 Peter 1:20–21)

This is Peter's way of saying that prophets do not just make stuff up. The prophetic word of Scripture is not based on a vague and loose interpretation of events. No prophecy, and no Scripture for that matter, originates in human imagination. Rather, the prophets—and we might just as well add apostles and evangelists here too—spoke from God as they were "carried along by the Holy Spirit." To be "carried along" does not mean a mechanical and overpowering sense, but more like being carried to the point of awareness and understanding. The prophetic word, whether spoken or written, is not a feat of human invention, but is attributed to the Spirit's power infused into the personality of the speaker or author.

Taking 2 Timothy 3:16 and 2 Peter 1:20–21 together, it seems that Scripture itself claims that biblical authors were divinely moved and spiritually endowed to receive a word from God and write it into human words. Scripture is *not merely* the record of divine revelation (though it is that). Scripture is *not merely* something to illuminate our minds with insights about God and his purposes (though it does that too!). Scripture itself *is* a revelation since God inspired his word into human subjects who were carried along by the Holy Spirit's influence to write a divinely given message. God's word consists of divine testimony to truth which was infused into people and then inscribed onto pages. This is what we are talking about when we discuss biblical inspiration.

HOW GOD MOVES AN AUTHOR TO WRITE SCRIPTURE

So far we've seen that Scripture is "God-breathed" and biblical authors were "carried along by the Holy Spirit." That's great, but what does it precisely mean? What happens when his breathing-out and carrying-along goes down? What does inspiration actually do to the minds and writing hands of the prophets, historians, sages, poets, editors, and apostles who wrote the Bible? Well, there are several possibilities to consider.

Inspiration as Artistic Ability

To begin with, some people consider biblical inspiration to be like artistic inspiration. Feelings of religious fervour, meditation on God, or basking in God's creation lead a person to verbalize their experience of what God is saying to them. This makes God more of a muse than a communicator. God inspires people in the same sense that a sunrise or a rose inspires a poet. But it is kind of absurd to imagine Moses thinking, "Gosh, I feel angry today. Maybe God is telling us to kill all the Canaanites," and then writing instructions on the conquest of Canaan (Deuteronomy 20:17). Or Matthew saying, "I feel really blessed today. I reckon Jesus would really want to bless lots of people," and then composing the Beatitudes (Matthew 5:1–12). Or Isaiah reflecting on the despair of Israel languishing in Babylon and feeling compelled by the idea of God's mercy to imagine a day when God rescues the exiles from Babylon and returns them to Judea (Isaiah 40–55). Divine inspiration should not be equated with religious feelings attributed to God or sensations of creativity that make God merely the stimulus of one's imagination.

Inspiration as Divine Endorsement

Others conceive of inspiration as God's validation of a written text. That is to say that Hosea and James composed their respective works, basically their own ideas written on their own steam, and then God simply put his heavenly stamp of approval on what they wrote. As if God said, "I'm God and I approve this message." But inspiration is not merely divine endorsement of a religious text. God is active in revelation rather than retrospectively affirming human literary projects. Such a view of inspiration reduces God to the role of a publishing editor, or even worse, a literary critic.

Inspiration as Divine Dictation

A common explanation for biblical inspiration has been divine dictation. In divine dictation, God speaks into the mind of an Obadiah or a Luke, who in turn write word-for-word what they hear. To be fair, there is something akin to dictation narrated in Scripture when God tells someone to write something down. For example, this happened when the Lord told Moses to write down the song of deliverance that the Israelites would sing as a memorial to what the Lord had done for them in the exodus (Deuteronomy 31:19–22). God instructed Isaiah to commit to writing a prophetic warning about the folly of looking to Egypt for deliverance from Assyria (Isaiah 30:8). Jeremiah is told on one occasion to "write in a book all the words I have spoken to you" (Jeremiah 30:2; also see 36:2, 28). Finally, John of Patmos is instructed to write certain words from the exalted Jesus in the first person to the churches of Ephesus, Smyrna, Pergamum, Thyatira, Sardis, Philadelphia, and Laodicea (Revelation 2:1, 8, 12, 18; 3:1, 7, 14; 14:13; 19:9; 21:5). However, while dictation might be seen in a few limited instances, it does not appear to have been normal. I don't think God dictated to Luke that he had to say that "I myself have carefully investigated everything from the beginning" if he didn't actually do that (Luke 1:3), nor did he dictate to Paul whom he forgot he baptized halfway through a sentence rebuking the Corinthians (1 Corinthians 1:14–16). I think Luke believed that he was writing something that he had carefully investigated, pondered, and crafted into an elegant historical narrative about Jesus and the early church, not just writing what God supernaturally downloaded into his brain word-for-word. In 1 Corinthians, Paul genuinely forgot whom he baptized and then backtracked midsentence—hard to imagine God dictating that to him. Also, if dictation occurred, then why are the biblical books in so many different styles, why do they use different vocabularies, and why do they exhibit the personalities of their authors so acutely? Dictation theory removes the human element of Scripture by denying that the personas of the authors shine through the texts. And, at the risk of sounding irreverent, if God dictated the Greek of the book of Revelation, then to be honest, God seriously needs some remedial grammar lessons because the Greek of Revelation is rough and clunky. So, a half-tick to dictation on a few occasions, but it will not do as the main explanation for what inspiration means since it negates the human dimension of Scripture.

Inspiration as Divine Enablement with Words

The most prevalent account of biblical inspiration among evangelical theologians is "plenary verbal inspiration." On this view, inspiration pertains to God's work to guide the minds and personalities of human authors so that they would freely choose to write in their own words the intended meaning of what God had revealed to them. This view is better than dictation theory because it permits a role for human personalities in the composition of Scripture and yet still makes God the ultimate author of the individual words written. However, one problem is that this seems like dictation theory by a slightly lesser degree. If plenary verbal inspiration still extends to words and word order of Scripture, how is this materially different from dictation theory?

Inspiration as the Incarnation of Divine Ideas in Human Words

There has been an attempt to articulate inspiration as something similar to the incarnation: a union of divine and human elements. On this view, Scripture is where God's word takes on the flesh of human language, so that the Bible is fully divine and fully human. Sounds good, but no, it will not do! Jesus is an incarnation of God, God in human flesh, the union of human and divine natures without confusion, change, mixing, or separation in the man Jesus of Nazareth. This is clearly *not* what happens during the composition of Scripture. Beyond that, let us remember too that the incarnation is unique; incarnation is not God's normal mode of self-communication. The revelation of a divine word through the mind of a human author is one thing, but the revelation of the Word of God as a human person in the flesh is quite another. God's word as a book and God's Word made flesh are both revelatory and redemptive, but they are not the same thing.

Catholic and evangelical theologians have used the incarnation as an analogy for inspiration. The 1942 papal encyclical *Divino Afflante Spiritu* says, "For as the substantial Word of God became like to men in all things, 'except sin,' so the words of God, expressed in human language, are made like to human speech in every respect, except error," and the 1982 Chicago Statement on Biblical Hermeneutics asserts that "we affirm that as Christ is God and Man in one Person, so Scripture is, indivisibly, God's Word in human language."

Inspiration as Conceptual Guidance

My view is that inspiration is principally God's guiding and leading human minds at the conceptual level, that is, general notions, broad ideas, the building blocks for words and sentences. Inspiration is how God, through the Holy Spirit, stimulates human minds at the level that the brain formulates ideas into words and sentences so that authors, through their experiences, learning, emotions, and words, write a message consistent with the divine intention. This is not to say that God simply gives an author the gist of what he wants them to say. As if God tells the psalmist to write something poetic about God as a Shepherd which leads him to write Psalm 23, or as if God gives Paul a few ideas about love which he then turns into the ode to love in 1 Corinthians 13. Rather, inspiration in this view is the direction of personal thinking. In its extent, inspiration directs thoughts, not the syllables of individual words. Inspiration involves a kind of supernatural connection between God's ideas and their verbal expression in the minds of the individual authors.

Envisaging inspiration as primarily a direction of a person's mental conceptions means that God's word is translatable. If inspiration applies to the original words of the Hebrew, Aramaic, and Greek, then it means that those words alone are the divine revelation. That would inescapably mean that our English Bibles are not the actual words of God, but a mere translation of them into English. Such a view of inspiration is explicitly taught in Islam where the Qu'ran in its original Arabic, and only in Arabic, is Allah's word. All subsequent translations of the Qu'ran are not equated with the divine revelation allegedly given to Muhammad by the angel Gabriel. Yet, if we regard inspiration as pertaining to God implanting ideas into the minds of human authors, rather than giving them actual words, then translations which express the same ideas and convey the same knowledge can be regarded as genuine expressions of God's word. Consequently, locating inspiration at a conceptual level rather than at the verbal level means that your English Bible is indeed the word of God.

The Why and How of the Inspiration

Two further things we need to mention are the **purposes** behind God's inspiration and the wider **processes** involved in the production of biblical books.

By breathing God's word into human minds and carrying human authors along by the Spirit, God is trying to tell us something and to do something to us by the very act of telling. God gives us his inspired word not just to inform us but to transform us. God's inspired word is not just facts for people but is intended to impact people. God's inspired word is not just statements searching for assent but speech calling for repentance, lament, joy, hope, pondering, determination, discipline, compassion, justice, and trust. God does not inspire authors to write tidbits of trivia to be filed away in the back of your mind for later retrieval. God inspires the biblical authors to compose a diverse array of genres like creation stories, ancient law codes, Hebrew poetry, prophecy, Gospels, epistles, and even an apocalypse in order to shape our minds and imaginations according to a God-centred worldview. God's inspired word achieves a myriad of effects best summarized as teaching, rebuking, correcting, and training in righteousness (2 Timothy 3:16). We will have more to say on the purpose of Scripture in chapter 6.

In addition, while inspiration might pertain to the Holy Spirit's imparting of ideas, the production of a scriptural text often involves a number of human processes that are directed by the Spirit's guidance. For instance, it is clear that certain books in the Bible were composed and compiled over a period of time, like the Pentateuch, which is a collection of legal traditions and stories that were probably edited by a group of priests sometime soon after the Babylonian exile. Then there are the Psalms, which is a collection of five books of psalms with individual psalms written by different authors, and with each book having its own distinctive themes and literary history. Other writings, like Isaiah, probably emerged in three distinct phases as Isaiah's prophecy was remembered, reinterpreted, and reinscribed over the course of the Assyrian (Isaiah 1–39), Babylonian (Isaiah 40–55), and Persian periods (Isaiah 56–66). The Gospel of John includes the evangelist's own conclusion (John 20:31), an epilogue subsequently attached (John 21:1–23), and a conclusion composed by the Gospel's editors (John 21:24–25). I tend to be cautious about certain theories of biblical books having been stitched together from multiple sources—as is often proposed for 2 Corinthians and Philippians—but in general there are good grounds for regarding some biblical books as a collective enterprise composed over some decades by an initial author and later editors. A high view of Scripture should embrace both the Holy Spirit's inspiration of authors as well as the Holy Spirit's "sanctification of creaturely processes," including guidance of the collection, editing, and canonization of ancient texts, which gave us Holy Scripture.[1]

DIVINE SPEECH THAT IS TRUE AND TRUSTWORTHY

The Inerrancy Debate

When God speaks through human authors, he brings his word to us, and it is a true word. God speaks the truth and he does not lie nor mislead us (see Numbers 23:19!). So we can expect Holy Scripture to be true because God has invested his own faithfulness and truthfulness in it.

---

1. John Webster, *Holy Scripture: A Dogmatic Sketch* (Cambridge: Cambridge University Press, 2003), 17.

But that still leads to questions about exactly how or to what extent Scripture is true. Is Scripture true even when it refers to scientific matters about the creation of the universe? Is it fully accurate on the fine historical details about the Israelites and the chronology of Jesus's life? Or are its truth claims restricted to theological matters like salvation, ethics, and church governance? Does Scripture contain any errors at all like errors of fact or errors of consistency? Can we say that the Bible is true in matters of faith but potentially in error in matters of science, biology, and history? That is what the inerrancy debates are over, and they can be particularly brutal affairs when played out in conservative Christian contexts.

STATEMENTS OF SCRIPTURE IN DIFFERENT CONFESSIONS AND DOCTRINAL STATEMENTS

- Anglican 39 Articles, article 6 (1571): "authority" and "sufficiency" of Scripture
- Westminster Confession 1.5 (1647): "infallible truth and divine authority"
- Armenian Evangelical Churches of Turkey (1846): "The Holy Spirit, our Comforter, who inspired the sacred scriptures of the Old and New Testaments, our supreme authority in all matters of faith and conduct."
- World Assembly of God Statement of Faith, article 2 (1916): The Bible is inspired by God and is "the infallible, authoritative rule of faith and conduct."

- Universities and Colleges Christian Fellowship, article 3 (1928): "The Bible, as originally given, is the inspired and infallible Word of God. It is the supreme authority in all matters of belief and behavior."
- National Association of Evangelicals Statement of Faith (1942): "We believe the Bible to be the inspired, the only infallible, authoritative Word of God."
- The Jerusalem Declaration of the Fellowship of Confessing Anglicans (2008): "We believe the Holy Scriptures of the Old and New Testaments to be the Word of God written and to contain all things necessary for salvation. The Bible is to be translated, read, preached, taught and obeyed in its plain and canonical sense, respectful of the church's historic and consensual reading."

Inerrancy Wars in Evangelicalism

In the history of American evangelicalism, especially in the last one hundred years, inerrancy has been the defining issue within the evangelical camp and has led to all sorts of debates, denominational breakups, and institutional divisions. Indeed, it is not too much to say that "inerrancy" holds a place, a priority, and a demand for precision in American churches that is simply absent in the rest of the world. Don't get me wrong, global evangelical churches do believe quite earnestly in the Bible's inspiration and infallibility, just not with the ardor or aggression that has been raging since the 1970s in American evangelicalism's "battle for the Bible."

Let me share a story that illustrates the ferocity of

American evangelical infighting over inerrancy and how it even led some evangelical conservatives to go cannibal on each other. I have a friend named Dr. Michael Licona, and he is a brilliant Christian apologist who has defended Christianity against critiques from atheists and Muslims. He is a great speaker and writer. He wrote a really good book on the historicity of the resurrection.[2] In that book, he had to deal with one especially tricky passage in Matthew's Gospel:

> At that moment the curtain of the temple was torn in two from top to bottom. The earth shook, the rocks split and the tombs broke open. The bodies of many holy people who had died were raised to life. They came out of the tombs after Jesus' resurrection and went into the holy city and appeared to many people. (Matthew 27:51–53)

Now, this text is odd because you have people, ancient Israelite saints, apparently being raised back to life, not just *before* the general resurrection of the dead at the end of history (see Daniel 12:1–2; John 5:29; 11:24; Acts 23:6, 8; 24:15, 21), but even *before* Jesus's own resurrection, which is very strange because Jesus's resurrection is supposed to be the "firstfruits" of the future resurrection (see 1 Corinthians 15:20–23). Plus, Matthew tells us that these holy people were raised to life when Jesus died but did not come out of their respective tombs until after Jesus's resurrection, which is a

---

2. Michael R. Licona, *The Resurrection of Jesus: A New Historiographical Approach* (Downers Grove, IL: InterVarsity Press, 2011).

kind of awkward intermission. What is more, if this literally happened, you'd think that maybe a Jewish historian like Josephus or a Roman historian like Tacitus might have mentioned this amazing event of ancient Israelite men and women coming back to life in Jerusalem, even if only temporarily. D. A. Carson appropriately labels this episode as "extraordinarily difficult."[3] So what is going on here?

Well, Licona comments that this really is a "strange little text" and he notes how many strange phenomena like earthquakes and cosmic portents were said to accompany the death of great leaders in ancient sources. Licona surmises:

> It seems to me that an understanding of the language in Matthew 27:52–53 as "special effects" with eschatological Jewish texts and thought in mind is most plausible. There is further support for this interpretation. If the tombs were opened and the saints being raised upon Jesus' death was not strange enough, Matthew adds that they did not come out of their tombs until *after* Jesus' resurrection. What were they doing between Friday afternoon and early Sunday morning? Were they standing in the now open doorways of their tombs and waiting?

Licona then regards "this difficult text in Mathew as a poetic device added to communicate that the Son of God

---

3. D. A. Carson, "Matthew," in *The Expositor's Bible Commentary: Matthew and Mark*, ed. T. Longman and D. E. Garland, rev. ed. (Grand Rapids: Zondervan, 2010), 650.

had died and that the impending judgment awaited Israel."[4] I agree with his interpretation; in fact, in an earlier publication I wrote: "My understanding of this text is that it is not historical and it blends the present and the future together, so that Matthew provides a cameo of the future resurrection at the point of Jesus' death to underscore its living-giving power."[5] Even if you disagree with such a line of interpretation, I hope you appreciate that Licona and I are both trying to come up with a defensible and sensible exegesis of this difficult Matthean text.

However, not everyone was politely disagreeable, and Licona found himself accused of denying the doctrine of biblical inerrancy. The "logic" of his critics was that if you don't believe in a literal resurrection in Matthew 27:52, then obviously you are at risk of denying that Jesus was literally raised to life in Matthew 28. As a result, Licona was denounced on various websites, had various speaking engagements cancelled, was disinvited from teaching at several colleges, and was treated as if he had written a book called *Why I Like to Worship Satan and Torture Cute Puppies*. I think Licona's view is entirely plausible and in accordance with historical Christian orthodoxy, and even if one does not agree with him in this particular instance, there was no excuse to treat him as the mother of all heretics.

Rather than offer an impassioned defense of Licona within American evangelicalism, I think the whole tragic episode warrants a few comments about the place

---

4. Licona, *Resurrection of Jesus*, 548, 552–53.
5. Michael F. Bird and James G. Crossley, *How Did Christianity Begin?: A Believer and Non-Believer Examine the Evidence* (London: SPCK, 2008), 69n.60.

of inerrancy within American evangelicalism (with relevance to other countries that have enclaves or satellites of American conservative evangelical culture):

1. For many American evangelicals, inerrancy is kind of like your passport and residency visa within the evangelical tribe; without it you can expect to get deported.

2. Although inerrancy can be defined in numerous ways[6]—and I can affirm a nuanced version of inerrancy[7]—inside American conservative evangelicalism one's bona fide credentials and doctrinal righteousness are determined by having the strictest and most wooden version of inerrancy. There appears to be among some evangelical leaders an ongoing rivalry that "I'm more inerrantist than thou and I can prove it by the number of people that I denounce."

3. Some people preach on the inerrancy of the *Scriptures*, but what they really mean is the inerrancy of *their interpretation* of Scripture. In other words, the battle for the Bible is not always about the Bible, it is really about the dominance of specific types of religious culture and the hegemony of key personalities within certain institutions.

---

6. See David S. Dockery, *The Doctrine of the Bible* (Nashville: Convention, 1991), 86–88; James Merrick and Stephen M. Garrett, eds., *Five Views on Biblical Inerrancy* (Grand Rapids: Zondervan, 2013).

7. See Michael F. Bird, "Inerrancy Is Not Necessary for Evangelicalism outside the USA," in *Five Views on Biblical Inerrancy*, ed. James Merrick and Stephen M. Garrett (Grand Rapids: Zondervan, 2013), 145–73; idem, *Evangelical Theology: A Biblical and Systematic Introduction* (Grand Rapids: Zondervan, 2013), 642–46.

4. On the topic of inerrancy, American evangelicals can be viciously tribal and chillingly cannibal on each other.

I find the whole American evangelical fixation on inerrancy and its bitter infighting so weird because outside of American evangelical subculture, among the global churches, no one treats inerrancy as *the* number one issue that separates the good guys from the bad guys. In the parts of the evangelical world that I've lived in and had contact with, the Bible is cherished, its truth is affirmed, and its authority is preserved by believers from Albania to Zimbabwe. However, in contrast to conservative evangelicals in North America, a cumbersome and strict definition of inerrancy has never been the central and defining feature of global evangelical churches. To be honest, if your church is being hunted by either Communists or the Caliphate, you don't have the luxury of splitting denominations over hairsplitting definitions of inerrancy. Context provides clarity as to what matters most in faith, worship, ministry, life, and death.

Thinking Wisely about Biblical Inerrancy

When it comes to developing an approach to define how the Bible is true, if we begin with the witness of Scripture to itself, then we see that God's word is truthful in all that it affirms. In the Psalms, we read things like "the words of the Lord are flawless, like silver purified in a crucible, like gold refined seven times" (Psalm 12:6); "the law of the Lord is perfect, refreshing the soul. The statutes of the Lord are trustworthy" (19:7); and "the word of the Lord is right and true; he is faithful in all he does" (Psalm 33:4). According to

John, Jesus himself said, "The Scripture cannot be broken" (John 10:35 ESV), meaning that Scripture cannot prove to be inconsistent with itself. John of Patmos constantly emphasized that the words of his prophecy are "trustworthy and true" (Revelation 21:5; 22:6) because they come from Jesus who is himself faithful, holy, just, and true (Revelation 3:7, 14; 15:3). The testimony of God's word to itself is that Scripture is an authentic and authoritative account of everything which it declares to have happened, to be, or will yet take place.

To be honest, here we must nuance things very carefully or we risk making indefensible claims about Scripture. It is important to stress that God's revelation in Scripture is *accommodated* to the worldview and expectations of its original audience in matters of the way the physical world works, the understanding of history, notions of literary genres, and standards of truth telling. That said, the accommodation is never a giving in to sheer error. God does not speak erroneously, nor does he feed us nuts of truth lodged inside shells of falsehood. So, for instance, I think that the Gospel of Luke and Acts of the Apostles is a reliable two-volume account of Jesus and the early church written according to the standards of historical accuracy that the author and readers knew. Luke-Acts, as scholars often refer to these books, is historically true within the bounds of what would have been expected of a purportedly historical narrative with clear theological goals and rhetorical flair to enhance the account. In a world without footnotes, quotation marks, or bibliographies, and which permitted some degree of artistic license in narrating history, we can be sure that Luke is a historian of the first rank.

Christian theologians have normally affirmed that Scripture is inspired, authoritative, and truthful. The Lausanne Covenant (1974) declares a belief shared by evangelicals around the world: "We affirm the divine inspiration, truthfulness and authority of both Old and New Testament Scriptures in their entirety as the only written word of God, without error in all that it affirms, and the only infallible rule of faith and practice."[8] Similarly, according to the Chicago Statement on Biblical Inerrancy (1979), "Scripture, having been given by divine inspiration, is infallible, so that, far from misleading us, it is true and reliable in all the matters it addresses. . . . Scripture in its entirety is inerrant, being free from all falsehood, fraud, or deceit."[9] Such statements by themselves are fine; the challenge is how one applies them to particular problems of history, science, and literature that the Bible occasionally throws up for us. Thus, while you can find fulsome statements of faith that regard Scripture as "infallible" (cannot err) or "inerrant" (does not err), and this is all well and good, nonetheless, these statements and their claims about Scripture can be problematic if they do not sufficiently help you convincingly address questions raised by reading Scripture.

These questions can include things like "Why is the Pentateuch attributed to Moses when it shows signs of being compiled long after Moses?" Or "How do we match modern understandings of the universe's origins with Genesis 1?" Or "Is the book of Jonah actual history or a type of extended parable?" My point is that *if* your doctrine of inerrancy

---

8. Lausanne Covenant, §2.
9. CSBI, §11–12.

means you cannot explain why the evangelists do not agree on the details of Jesus's entrance into Jericho, *then* your inerrancy model will not last the winter of its own peculiarities or survive the summer of simple queries. Did Jesus heal *one* blind man on the way *out of* Jericho (Mark 10:46) or on the way *into* Jericho (Luke 18:35), or was it *two* blind men (Matthew 20:29–30)? Can you address these issues without fanciful suggestions like Jesus healed one blind man on the way into Jericho and two blind men on the way out of Jericho? Or can we accept that the evangelists felt free to amend the details in the storytelling? By seeking to define the precise way in which Scripture is true, or not untrue, you risk defining it so narrowly that the first time you find something in Scripture that does not seem to fit, you end up having to choose between a true Bible and a falsified Bible. Inerrancy should not be posed as an alternative to unbelief. As if one is asked: Do you believe in *either* (a) biblical inerrancy with Mosaic authorship of the Pentateuch, six literal twenty-four-hour days of creation, the historical existence of Jonah and Job, that all the psalms were written by David, the four Gospels were written independently, Paul wrote Hebrews, and the book of Revelation should be interpreted in a strictly literal fashion; *or* (b) a bunch of atheist, Marxist, liberal, secularized, Christ-hating, sacrilegious blasphemy of God's holy word? Trust me, there is an option (c), which I'm trying to lay out for you. Be that as it may, well intentioned as some are in trying to fortify their own doctrine of Scripture with naked assertions of its truthfulness and how it is true, they can inadvertently shatter other people's confidence in the Bible and even shipwreck their faith.

A healthy doctrine of Scripture, with a cogent and careful definition of inerrancy, should not deny apparent ambiguities nor mute anyone's gnawing questions. There are even types of errors that one can accept if you understand divine accommodation to ancient worldviews and how ancient literary genres work (such as the evangelists tinkering with the story about Jesus healing a blind man in Jericho). Admitting such a fact in no way undermines the truthfulness and authority of Scripture. Inerrancy can be retained as long as it has certain qualifications, nuances, and thick explanations. In those explanations we affirm the phenomenon of Scripture, the divine and human elements of Scripture, the progressive nature of revelation where the new supersedes the old, and God's accommodation to the ancient worldviews in Scripture. In other words, you can't explain inerrancy or infallibility using terse descriptions, like answers to a multiple-choice test. Instead, you need an essay on God as a revealing God, the meaning of inspiration, and more in order to properly explain what is and is not being claimed. Some might complain that this means that inerrancy or infallibility dies the death of a thousand qualifications. Well, perhaps, but trust me, any complex term, whether it is "democracy" or "incarnation," is going to need layers of explanation if the concept is to be properly understood and not knocked down as a flimsy straw-man argument. Some ideas in theology and religion are irreducibly complex. Anything related to truth claims and the Bible is bound to be so. So, when it comes to describing infallibility and inerrancy, if you ask me, bigger books are actually better.

JESUS'S HEALING OF THE BLIND MAN/MEN IN JERICHO

Matthew 20:29–34	[29]As Jesus and his disciples were leaving Jericho, a large crowd followed him. [30]Two blind men were sitting by the roadside, and when they heard that Jesus was going by, they shouted, "Lord, Son of David, have mercy on us!" [31]The crowd rebuked them and told them to be quiet, but they shouted all the louder, "Lord, Son of David, have mercy on us!" [32]Jesus stopped and called them. "What do you want me to do for you?" he asked. [33]"Lord," they answered, "we want our sight." [34]Jesus had compassion on them and touched their eyes. Immediately they received their sight and followed him.
Mark 10:46–52	[46]Then they came to Jericho. As Jesus and his disciples, together with a large crowd, were leaving the city, a blind man, Bartimaeus (which means "son of Timaeus"), was sitting by the roadside begging. [47]When he heard that it was Jesus of Nazareth, he began to shout, "Jesus, Son of David, have mercy on me!" [48]Many rebuked him and told him to be quiet, but he shouted all the more, "Son of David, have mercy on me!" [49]Jesus stopped and said, "Call him." So they called to the blind man, "Cheer up! On your feet! He's calling you." [50]Throwing his cloak aside, he jumped to his feet and came to Jesus. [51]"What do you want me to do for you?" Jesus asked him. The blind man said, "Rabbi, I want to see." [52]"Go," said Jesus, "your faith has healed you." Immediately he received his sight and followed Jesus along the road.
Luke 18:35–43	[35]As Jesus approached Jericho, a blind man was sitting by the roadside begging. [36]When he heard the crowd going by, he asked what was happening. [37]They told him, "Jesus of Nazareth is passing by." [38]He called out, "Jesus, Son of David, have mercy on me!" [39]Those who led the way rebuked him and told him to be quiet, but he shouted all the more, "Son of David, have mercy on me!" [40]Jesus stopped and ordered the man to be brought to him. When he came near, Jesus asked him, [41]"What do you want me to do for you?" "Lord, I want to see," he replied. [42]Jesus said to him, "Receive your sight; your faith has healed you." [43]Immediately he received his sight and followed Jesus, praising God. When all the people saw it, they also praised God.

What Makes the Bible a True Book?

What is the basis for belief in the Bible as inspired, infallible, and inerrant? Well, "the Bible itself says so" is one such argument, but that is a remarkably circular way of putting it and it will not satisfy a lot of people. Alternatively, one could try to prove the historicity of the Bible from the age of the patriarchs through to the ministry of the apostles, but that itself is not a surefire strategy, and it can raise more questions than it solves.

For my money, ultimately, if Scripture is God's own word, then its truthfulness is safeguarded, not by our efforts to harmonize any apparent inconsistency or even in our sophisticated arguments to prove the absence of error. Rather, scriptural truthfulness is simply the outworking of God's faithfulness.[10] That is to say, the truthfulness of Scripture is grounded in the faithfulness of God to his own word. Unsurprisingly, this is precisely what we find repeated in Psalm 119 and Revelation 21–22: God's word is truthful because it reflects the truthfulness of God himself.

What makes Scripture compelling to us is the Holy Spirit's testimony. As the Westminster Confession says, "Our full persuasion and assurance of the infallible truth and divine authority thereof, is from the inward work of the Holy Spirit bearing witness by and with the Word in our hearts."[11] That derives from Jesus's own words that the Holy Spirit "will guide you into all the truth" (John 16:13). Scripture is authenticated through the witness of the Spirit

---

10. Carl Trueman and Paul Helm, eds., *The Trustworthiness of God: Perspectives on the Nature of Scripture* (Grand Rapids: Eerdmans, 2002).

11. WCF §1.5.

of God that tells us that God's word can be trusted. The Bible is God's word not because we have "evidence that demands a verdict," nor because of any church council that said so, but on account of the witness of the Holy Spirit to our spirit that we are reading the true words of a truthful God in Holy Scripture. All other evidence, from apologetics or historical theology, is secondary to the work of the Holy Spirit in authoring and authenticating Scripture.

RECOMMENDED READING

Inspiration

Marshall, I. Howard. *Biblical Inspiration*. Milton Keynes, UK: Paternoster, 2005.

McGowan, Andrew. *The Divine Authenticity of Scripture: Retrieving Evangelical Heritage*. Downers Grove, IL: InterVarsity Press, 2008.

Ward, Timothy. *Words of Life: Scripture as the Living and Active Word of God*. Downers Grove, IL: InterVarsity Press, 2014.

Inerrancy

Carson, D. A., ed. *The Enduring Authority of the Christian Scriptures*. Grand Rapids: Eerdmans, 2016.

Garrett, Stephen M., and James Merrick, eds. *Five Views of Biblical Inerrancy*. Grand Rapids: Zondervan, 2013.

3

SCRIPTURE
IS NORMATIVE,
NOT NEGOTIABLE

After having looked at ideas of biblical inspiration and biblical truthfulness in the previous chapter, we are now set to examine the topic of biblical authority. In some ways this is not a separate topic because the Bible's authority is indelibly connected to the belief that it is God-given and completely trustworthy. The Bible is a word from God and is true, and thus it contains the weight of divine authority. But—and here's where the debate starts—how precisely is the Bible an authority and how do you live under such authority? Is the Bible equally authoritative and therefore prescriptive in all its parts? How do we separate God's authority, biblical authority, and the authority of the interpreter? As we'll see, the notion of biblical authority can be contentious in both theory and practice.

THE MEANING OF
BIBLICAL AUTHORITY

The dividing line between traditional, historical, and ortho-dox Christianity and liberal, progressive Christianity is not about being pro- or anti-inerrancy. The real issue is whether the Bible is in any sense prescriptive for Christian faith. For many liberal Christians and progressive churches, the Bible is not **normative** in any way; rather, it is **negotiable** in every place. In most mainline churches, the Bible is not definitive for the religious life of the churches; everything the Bible teaches is up for debate, compromise, and negotiation. In the minds of many mainline Christians, to treat the Bible as authoritative would turn it into a "Paper Pope" or require joining a fundamentalist movement—both of which strike them with revulsion. In some cases, I understand what they are afraid of or allergic to, but it is hard to regard this attitude as anything other than a naked denial of divine authority operating through Scripture. In many churches today and according to many contemporary theologians, the Bible at best provides some good sound bites for a few sociopolitical projects one has going on.

I am not making this up, so let me prove it to you by pointing to a tweet from Union Seminary. Union is a mainline seminary in New York City, whose Twitter account had some rather provocative thoughts on the role of the Bible in Christianity. According to Union Seminary: "While divinely inspired, we deny the Bible is inerrant or infallible. It was written by men over centuries and thus reflects both God's truth and human sin & prejudice.

> The authority of Scripture is a key issue for the Christian Church in this and every age. Those who profess faith in Jesus Christ as Lord and Savior are called to show the reality of their discipleship by humbly and faithfully obeying God's written Word. To stray from Scripture in faith or conduct is disloyalty to our Master. Recognition of the total truth and trustworthiness of Holy Scripture is essential to a full grasp and adequate confession of its authority.
>
> —*Chicago Statement on Biblical Inerrancy, preface*

We affirm that biblical scholarship and critical theory help us discern which messages are God's."[1] For those who don't speak progressive-ese, let me translate that for you:

> The Bible has some bits that genuinely come from God and other bits that represent human prejudice and bigotry. Thanks to the invention of "critical theory," a postmodern literary approach that teaches that all claims to truth are in reality claims to power, that everyone can be divided into either "oppressor" or "oppressed," we can identify the divine bits of the Bible and the oppressive bits that are products of capitalist, patriarchal, heteronormative, racist, Zionist, and alt-right evil. No one else in church history was able to do this before us, because the churches of previous ages were filled with insidiously evil cisgender white males, so we

---

1. @UnionSeminary, September 6, 2018, https://twitter.com/unionseminary/status/1037346517936472070?lang=en.

really are the ones the church has been waiting for, since only we have the privileged progressive perspective to show everyone which bits of the Bible actually come from God.

Strangely enough, the bits of the Bible that come from God just so happen to conform to politically progressive views on climate policy, immigration, socialism, gender fluidity, healthcare, abortion, religious freedom, education, geopolitical views of the EU and UN, and military expenditure—what an amazing coincidence!

Alas, there is nothing new under the sun (Ecclesiastes 1:9). The second-century arch-heretic Marcion stripped the Bible of anything Jewish, Thomas Jefferson cut out all the miracles, and now Union Seminary consigns all the non-progressive bits to the dumpster of "human sin & prejudice." As you might now appreciate, those of us who live outside the canopy of North American evangelicalism really cannot be bothered with the tribal debates of "I'm more inerrantist than thou" when we find the real threat to be churches and leaders who think the Bible is some kind of religious cadaver that needs to have its progressive organs surgically removed from its body. I'm not remotely worried that someone prefers "soft" inerrancy over "hard" inerrancy; I'm more anxious about my church and students being seduced by a view of Scripture that implies that God only speaks in the bits of Scripture that agree with a particular political ideology, whether that is the identity politics of the radical left or the syncretistic mix of nationalism and civil religion of the religious right. I do not want my students and church friends to end up treating the Bible as an antiquated spiritual text that can be used as needed to provide religious capital to whatever social and political projects they support.

One of the biggest challenges for the church today is not the erosion of inerrancy among millennial Christians; more seriously, it is whether the Bible is in any sense authoritative at all. The one thing the Union Seminary tweet does rightly raise is the issue of whether the Bible is truly authoritative for belief, church life, and ethics, or whether its vision for the life of faith is negotiable. I would say that treating the Bible as God's word, a word that is authoritative, normative, and to be obeyed, is the *evangelical view*. We evangelical Christians should maintain this idea of biblical authority as the touchstone for a healthy doctrine of Scripture rather than investing all our theological capital in a pedantic definition of how the Bible is not untrue. As John Stott wrote, "The hallmark of authentic evangelicalism is not subscription but submission. That is, it is not whether we subscribe to an impeccable formula about the Bible, but whether we live in practical submission to what the Bible teaches, including an advance resolve to submit to whatever it may later be shown to teach."[2] Amen to that!

What I want to do next is show why regarding the Bible as authoritative is challenging and complicated, and then show how a nuanced view of authority can still be maintained.

---

2. John Stott, *Evangelical Truth: A Personal Plea for Unity, Integrity, and Faithfulness* (Downers Grove, IL: InterVarsity Press, 1999), 73–74.

THE CHALLENGE OF BIBLICAL AUTHORITY FOR THE TWENTY-FIRST CENTURY

Why Biblical Authority Is Not Straightforward

It has been a while since I've seen one, but there really are people with bumper stickers on their car that say, "The Bible says it, I believe it, that settles it!" For many Christians, the Bible is simply God's word; God's word gives us either examples to follow or commands to obey, so the whole Bible is *prescriptive* and *authoritative*. We are supposed to obey it, live by it, follow its teachings, and keep in step with it. Sounds straightforward, but alas, there are several problems with that view. Consider the following biblical texts.

> One of the challenges of using the Bible for ethics is determining when a value is culturally bound and when it's enduring.
> —*Karen R. Keen*, Scripture, Ethics, and the Possibility of Same-Sex Relationships (*Grand Rapids: Eerdmans, 2018*), xx.

Most people I know are appalled by the jihadist group ISIS taking captured Christian and Yazidi women as sex slaves. But do you know that the Old Testament prescribes a similar practice when it comes to conquering a town or territory? If an Israelite man takes a foreign woman captive after a round of intertribal warfare, there is a grace period for her to mourn the desolation of her home and the butchering of her family, but after that, she is fair game as a "wife" of sorts.

When you go to war against your enemies and the LORD your God delivers them into your hands and you take captives, if you notice among the captives a beautiful woman and are attracted to her, you may take her as your wife. Bring her into your home and have her shave her head, trim her nails and put aside the clothes she was wearing when captured. After she has lived in your house and mourned her father and mother for a full month, then you may go to her and be her husband and she shall be your wife. If you are not pleased with her, let her go wherever she wishes. You must not sell her or treat her as a slave, since you have dishonored her. (Deuteronomy 21:10–14)

Or can you imagine a victim of rape being forced to marry her rapist? Yet that is what is explicitly commanded in Holy Scripture:

If a man happens to meet a virgin who is not pledged to be married and rapes her and they are discovered, he shall pay her father fifty shekels of silver. He must marry the young woman, for he has violated her. He can never divorce her as long as he lives. (Deuteronomy 22:28–29)

We can also identify some of the really weird commandments like "Do not wear clothes of wool and linen woven together" (Deuteronomy 22:11), "Do not cook a young goat in its mother's milk" (Exodus 23:19), and "Do not cut the hair at the sides of your head or clip off the edges of your beard" (Leviticus 19:27). No one, except perhaps an

Orthodox Jew, would think of obeying these commands today. Most Christians I know wear hybrid clothes and eat either cheeseburgers or curried goat cooked with cream, and most men I know tend to get a short-back-and-sides haircut! Stranger still, if a man suspects that his wife is having an adulterous relationship but cannot prove it, the Bible commands that he take his wife to see the priest for a test. The priest would sweep some dust off the floor of the tabernacle, mix it with some water, and then compel the wife to drink it. Now, if the concoction didn't make the woman sick, then she would be declared innocent, but if her stomach became bloated and painful, then she was declared guilty of adultery (Numbers 5:11–31).

Even the New Testament is not immune to some strange precedents and odd commandments. The apostles cast lots to find a replacement for Judas Iscariot, not exactly how I recommend churches decide between candidates for a pastoral position (Acts 1:26). Paul can say that "every man who prays or prophesies with his head covered dishonors his head. But every woman who prays or prophesies with her head uncovered dishonors her head—it is the same as having her head shaved." Such a commandment is rooted in creation since "a man ought not to cover his head, since he is the image and glory of God; but woman is the glory of man. For man did not come from woman, but woman from man." Paul even argues that this is universally practiced in all the churches he knows: "If anyone wants to be contentious about this, we have no other practice—nor do the churches of God" (1 Corinthians 11:4–8, 16). Finally, Peter also commands slaves to obey their masters, even the harsh ones, which in reality meant the ones who beat them, sexually used them, or sold their children to a brothel (1 Peter 2:18).

Put yourself in the position of an unchurched millennial for a moment. If you read this material for the first time, would you think that the Bible is (a) a sourcebook for family values and (b) God's will to be obeyed at all times? Probably not! The Bible is a sacred text that commands genocide, sanctions slavery, permits the sexual exploitation of slaves, and enables patriarchy and polygamy. Some people will also think it arbitrary that Christians do not obey the Levitical commandments about abstaining from pork and bacon (Leviticus 11:7) and yet think that the Levitical prohibition on homosexuality should remain in force today (Leviticus 18:22). In light of that, "The Bible says it, I believe it, that settles it" is somewhere between grossly naïve, utterly impractical, and positively horrible to imagine.

At this point, one could say that the Bible is so foreign, so distant, so weird, and so morally reprehensible to our sensitivities that it is not and cannot be authoritative. To get out of obeying the stuff in the Bible that you find repulsive or irrelevant, there are a few options from which you could choose:

1. Just dump the Old Testament in its entirety, then presto, most of the problems are gone. But no, we cannot do that, because Jesus and the apostles affirmed the Old Testament, and the Old Testament is an essential component in our account of God and the Christian faith.

2. Divide the Old Testament laws into civil, ceremonial, and moral components, with the civil and ceremonial aspects fulfilled by Christ, and the moral law signified by the Ten Commandments as remaining in full effect. Great way to dodge some of that strange stuff in the Old Testament! But it won't do either. The law is the law, an indissoluble unity; it cannot be neatly carved up into artificial categories, with some parts haphazardly disregarded. Plus, there are a whole bunch of moral laws outside the Ten Commandments that are affirmed in the New Testament.

3. Interpret the weird and disturbing parts of the Bible allegorically or spiritually. Again, no: while Scripture can have a deeper spiritual sense, this is a cheap copout that tries to avoid the problem by an interpretive sleight of hand.

4. Give up any notion of authority and just use the Bible as needed for our pet causes, from ending human trafficking to fighting poverty, and maybe use it as a guideline, not a rule book, on how to organize a religious community. An attractive option for some, but no: God's word is a lamp and guide to our feet, not a buffet of religious ideas we can pick and choose from.

What are we to do? It is problematic to regard the whole Bible as *directly* authoritative and *immediately* applicable. Consequently, if we are going to maintain the authority of the Bible, then we need to sufficiently grasp how biblical authority works when dealing with the more problematic parts of the Bible. My next task is to explain how.

WHY THE BIBLE IS NOT
ALWAYS AUTHORITATIVE

Some key factors help us negotiate the difficult parts of Scripture without rejecting biblical authority. I'll be honest, I am not promising that these factors solve every historical, moral, and canonical problem, but they do help us understand that while the Bible is indeed authoritative, **not everything in the Bible is authoritative for us**. What I'm going to do is argue that (1) we need to distinguish between what is prescriptive and descriptive; (2) many biblical commands are not applicable to us; (3) the Bible often trades in brutal realities and not ideal situations; (4) all biblical commands need to be situated in light of the progressive nature of divine revelation; (5) we must recognize the unique and final authority of Jesus; and (6) church doctrines can be understood as subject to revision as the church persistently seeks God's wisdom on matters of faith and practice.

Distinguish between What Is Prescriptive
and What Is Descriptive

The Bible often describes things that happened that are not meant to be replicated by us—in fact, sometimes it's clear that even the narrator doesn't think it was a good idea at the time! I really do not recommend pimping out your wife to a local ruler to save your own skin as Abraham did with Sarah (Genesis 12:11–20). Jephthah the Gileadite, one of Israel's judges, stupidly swore an oath to God that if God helped him defeat the Ammonites, then when he returned home, he would kill the first thing that met him as a burnt offering; sadly, it was his daughter, and it did not end well for her (Judges 11:30–40). I am also not sure if we should try to heal people with impaired eyesight like Jesus did by putting his saliva into someone's eyes since that was a unique event in Jesus's unique ministry (Mark 8:23–26). So note this: some parts of the Bible are not normative and were never designed to be repeated.

Grasp That Many Commands in the Bible Are Not Directly Relevant to Us

Some parts of the Bible were dealing with a specific problem and therefore are not directly applicable to our situation. If you read Acts 15, you'll notice that the apostolic decree from the Jerusalem Council gives gentile believers this instruction: "You are to abstain from food sacrificed to idols, *from blood*, from the meat of strangled animals and from sexual immorality. You will do well to avoid these things" (Act 15:29). One could conceivably infer from this—and I've even heard preachers say so—that Christians cannot eat their steak medium rare, that is, with blood still in it, because it violates the apostolic decree. We must remember though that the Jerusalem Council was about establishing a consensus on whether gentiles had to be circumcised and become converts to Judaism in order to join the church. The verdict of the Jerusalem Council—after hearing Peter's testimony and thanks to James's mediation—was that gentiles did not have to be circumcised to be followers of Jesus. However, to placate that wing of the Jerusalem church that regarded all things gentile with suspicion, the apostolic decree required gentile believers to abstain from sexual deviancy and food associated with idol worship. The point was not abstaining from blood because blood was just plain wrong to eat, but because of how blood was used in pagan rituals and sacrifices. So feel free to go to the Outback Steakhouse, order a Melbourne porterhouse medium rare, and eat it to the glory of God. Not because one is playing fast and loose with divine commands, but because not all commands are equally valid across the sweep of redemptive history. What you should remember is that some parts of the Bible were indeed authoritative back then, but because we live in a different context, under a different covenant, they are not applicable for us now.

Understand That the Biblical Stories and Commandments Deal with Harsh Realities, Not Necessarily Ideal Situations

There is the world as we would like it to be, and then there is the world as it is. In an ideal world, women are never subject to sexism, black people don't experience racism, and politicians are honest and transparent. However, the world is not ideal; the real world is cold, brutal, and dark. Or, as Amos and Paul said, "The days are evil" (Amos 5:13; Ephesians 5:16). As a result, we must deal with a world where women experience abuse and discrimination, where racism happens, and where corruption is common. We can expose injustice and strive for change, but in the interim, we have to be smart and do what we have to do in order to endure calamity and work for a better world. Jesus taught us to pray, "[Lord] . . . deliver us from evil" (Matthew 6:13 ESV), but when evil does come, he told us to "be as shrewd as snakes and as innocent as doves" (Matthew 10:16), and "if you don't have a sword, sell your cloak and buy one" (Luke 22:36). Sometimes the good guys wear grey, sometimes we have to live with moral ambiguity, sometimes the alternatives are not black and white, and sometimes even doing the right thing is merely doing the least ugly option.

Similarly, the Bible deals with the world as it is, in its cruelty and moral chaos. A world with intertribal warfare, marauders, judges who take bribes, famine, foreign empires, pagan religions, slavery, curses, infanticide, exploitation, and patriarchy. Thankfully God spoke his word into the context of the ancient Near East and into the Greco-Roman Mediterranean; it was a gracious word that dealt with the harsh realities of human existence, and it alleviated the misery of many. Yet, even as the divine word made things better, it did not always make things immediately perfect. The Bible speaks to a world that is messed up, and God's decrees for that world do not clean up every mess instantaneously. As such, the Bible's mandates were not always working within an ideal situation to begin with; rather, they were expedient for the environment that God's people inhabited at that time. God's commands to the Israelites about war, slaves, women, and justice made things incrementally better than they were, but not exactly perfect if judged by the standards of the New Testament or the Universal Declaration of Human Rights.

Let me put it like this. In God's ideal world, we beat swords into ploughshares. But in the cutthroat world of Canaan, a millennium before Christ, God's instructions told them what they had to do to survive if they went to war with the Ammonites, how they were to treat the survivors, how they were to make a treaty with a foreign people, how they were to stop foreign religions and cultures from taking over their own, how they were to treat someone who committed murder, etc. A lot of what we find in the Bible, especially in the Old Testament, is not ideal, at least not ideal when judged from the perspective of the New Testament. It was somewhere between an emergency survival program and an attempt to ameliorate a terrible and traumatic situation. The Old Testament conveys the ruthless realism of God's people trying to survive in the ancient world and dealing with a world that had a particular view of masculinity, kinship, moral duties, and social order. When we read the texts about war—including rhetorical tirades to show hostile tribes "no mercy" and the permissibility of taking women as captives—we need to imagine this God putting on a hazmat suit and trying to lead Israel through the toxic morass of human evil and taking them, incrementally, toward a better way of being human. We should read the Old Testament commands and stories about war knowing that war was for a particular purpose at a particular time and in a particular place, but it was not ideal, it was regrettable, it was ugly, but something better was coming.[3]

For us today, thankfully, Jesus has come and has not only brought with him God's truest purposes for our world but also launched this new world, the kingdom of God,

---

3. Here I am indebted to William J. Webb and Gordon K. Oeste, *Bloody, Brutal, and Barbaric: Wrestling with Troubling War Texts* (Downers Grove, IL: InterVarsity Press, 2019).

in which God's love and goodness defeat all evils and will one day make all things new. From our place, on the other side of Easter and Pentecost, we have the teaching of Jesus as something not only ideal but meant to be real for us in our own life and faith and made real again as we negotiate our own complex twenty-first-century world. I write this paragraph at the height of the COVID-19 emergency, and the churches are busy discerning within their own consciences how "to act justly and to love mercy and to walk humbly with your God" (Micah 6:8) and how to "love one another" as Jesus commanded (John 13:34–35). It has been hard work, I can tell you. Accordingly, one urgent task for today's church is to constantly think how, in the name of Christ, we can use the resources of our faith, our Scriptures, our traditions, as well as science, medicine, common justice, and shared human experience to make the world a better place. We are not trying to build some kind of secular utopia with a church on the corner. Our project is the kingdom of God, and yet it is God and God alone who ushers in God's kingdom, for the kingdom is not something we can ever manufacture by ourselves. But we can build *for* the kingdom by addressing the world with God's message of justice and love, the offer of reconciliation and forgiveness, and the compassion of Christ, and by using biblical notions of righteousness, equality, and charity to bring our fellow humans to their true identity as bearers of God's image. It is by doing that, with faithfulness and integrity, seeking the favour of God and our neighbours, that we most clearly put ourselves under the authority of God, the Holy Scriptures, and the teachings of Jesus Christ.

Interpret the Bible in Light of Progressive Revelation

One interpretive rule we need to remember is that God's revelation in Christ is the climax of God's revelation to us and represents the definitive account of God's purposes for us. That does not mean that everything before it is redundant or relativized, but it does mean that everything must be reviewed through the lens of God's continuous purpose for his people.

So, on the one hand, polygamy was tolerated and regulated in the Old Testament, largely out of practical necessity. Polygamy was a way to preserve tribal purity, to create familial and military alliances, and to maximize reproduction during a time with high mortality rates. Although, unsurprisingly, in most cases polygamy ended very badly for its practitioners, as it did for Abraham, Jacob, and Solomon. On the other hand, the ideal spelled out in Genesis is that marriage should be built around a husband-wife relationship (Genesis 2:24), which Jesus affirmed with the added emphasis that marriage is to the exclusion of all other relationships (Matthew 19:5–6), and Paul likewise reinforces marriage as one man and one woman (Ephesians 5:31–33; 1 Timothy 3:2). This means that you cannot read Genesis 16, where Sarah urges Abraham to take Hagar as his concubine, and say to yourself, "Well, Abraham had more than one woman. I'm a child of Abraham. So let's add a plus-one to this marriage," then log on to Tinder and start looking at king-sized beds at Mattress Depot. Sorry, no, polygamy might have been normal for the nomadic tribesman whom God chose to begin his rescue project, but it was not the ideal, and Jesus and Paul both spell out God's definitive word on marriage: it is a two-person show, one man and one woman.

Christians also need to understand that the Law of Moses was never intended as an eternal, for-now-and-forever, unchangeable series of divine commands to be obeyed always. Rather, the Mosaic covenant was a temporary administration of God's grace to govern Israel and was intended to cocoon God's promises around Israel until the promised messianic seed came. It taught the Israelites about God's holiness and the severity of sin; it deepened their capacity to worship God in a pagan environment. The Law pointed ahead to the coming of a messianic deliverer and was preparatory for Israel's role to extend salvation to the world. The Law was part of the scaffolding to keep things temporarily in order, upright, and stable, pointing ahead to a future world. But when the future came, the scaffolding was no longer required, because the new building was finished.

While the whole question of the abiding validity of the Law of Moses divides Christians, I'd argue that the Mosaic Law, even if distilled down to the Ten Commandments, is *not* the definitive summary of Christian ethics. Rather, the content of Christian ethics is the teaching of Jesus, the example of Jesus, and life in the Spirit. The Law remains relevant in many ways, but not as laws to be obeyed as such; rather, the Law remains relevant as a form of wisdom for Christian living, and a prophetic witness to Christ. In other words, the Law is more of a consultant for ethics than a code of ethics.[4]

---

4. See Brian S. Rosner, *Paul and the Law: Keeping the Commandments of God* (Downers Grove, IL: InterVarsity Press, 2013).

So, when we are faced with a problematic text about anything from polygamy to prohibitions on pork, we have to ask if it has been superseded by something better in God's progressive revelation of himself. We should recognize that the Mosaic Law is not the primary basis for Christian ethics, even while it remains a form of wisdom for Christian living. Biblical authority must be understood in light of God's progressive revelation climaxing in Jesus and the teaching of the apostles. It's called the *Old* Testament for a reason. Note, I did not call it the *Ugh, Gross* Testament. Not the *Well-We-Tried-That-but-It-Sucked* Testament. Not even the *Very Ancient and Strangely Jewish* Testament. The *Old* was good, it has its place and purpose, but it is supplanted by the *New*, even as the *New* affirms much of the *Old*.

Recognize the Unique Authority of Jesus

All Scripture is authoritative. However, special authority is to be associated with the teachings of Jesus. It should come as no surprise that the apostolic fathers and the apologists of the second century quoted from the Gospels more than any other part of Scripture. The early churches were in effect "red-letter Christians," who frequently quoted the words of Jesus as their first grounds of theological appeal and moral exhortation. The church's first theologians took their main theological impetus from the words of the Lord Jesus himself as recounted in the Gospels.

I'm keenly aware that this can be taken in a very irresponsible direction that plays Jesus off against the Bible. As if to say, "Who cares about what that cruel and merciless God of the Old Testament says—we have Jesus!"

or "Who cares what a misogynistic homophobe like Paul prattles on about—we have Jesus!" No, that's an affront to Jesus who affirmed the enduring authority of Israel's Scriptures, who authorized the apostles, who lives and reigns through his church, and who gave his disciples the keys to the kingdom to "bind" and "loose" as the Spirit led them (see Matthew 16:19; 18:18; John 20:23).

Instead, we should read the Old Testament the way Jesus taught us to: centred on his life, work, and teaching (Luke 24:44–45). We should always give special precedent to the teaching of Jesus on any topic, for ultimately, it is his word that is the final arbiter on truth, love, and the way of righteousness. The best clue to what is authoritative and applicable should come from teachings of the Lord Jesus himself (more on this to come in chapter 7).

Revise Doctrine as Revelation Requires

At no point in Christian tradition has theology ever been finished or frozen; it is always under construction as the church struggles to know its own mind while it attends to Scripture, wrestles with tradition, observes nature, reflects on experience, and speaks relevantly within its native cultures. The doctrine of the Trinity and ethics prohibiting slavery are exemplars of how Christian theology has developed.

The Trinity is not explicitly taught in the Bible as much as it is a biblical concept that emerged among the church fathers to enable the churches to make sense of what the Bible says about God and what the Bible implies about the relationships between the divine persons. The Trinity is how we explain that the Father is God, Jesus is God, and the Spirit is God, that there is one God not three gods, and that other solutions like modalism (one god with three faces) and subordinationism (Son and Spirit are lesser divinities than the Father) are not coherent explanations of God according to Scripture, worship, and experience. The doctrine of the Trinity developed, by necessity, from the church's reflection on Scripture, but it took some time to get there.

WHAT IS THE TRINITY?

According to the Westminster Confession of Faith, "In the unity of the Godhead there be three Persons of one substance, power, and eternity: God the Father, God the Son, and God the Holy Ghost. The Father is of none, neither begotten nor proceeding; the Son is eternally begotten of the Father; the Holy Ghost eternally proceeding from the Father and the Son" (WCF 2.3), and the Trinity is biblical in the sense that we regard the Trinity as a "good and necessary consequence [which] may be deduced from Scripture" (WCF 1.6).

The Bible assumes a world where slavery happens, where it is normal even if it is regrettable. There are exhortations to slaves on how to negotiate their difficult circumstances, a censuring of the abusive treatment of slaves, but no explicit call for the emancipation of all slaves. However, if one considers how a doctrine of the image of God provides seeds which can flower into notions about human rights

(Genesis 1:26–27; 9:6); if one meditates on a pro-equality text like Galatians 3:28 that affirms the equality of slave and free in Christ; if one considers Paul's exhortation for Philemon to receive Onesimus as a brother and not as a slave (Philemon 15–16); and if one remembers Paul's prohibition on a believer being a slave trader (1 Timothy 1:10), then banning slavery could be said to be a natural consequence of Christian teaching.

George Bourne, an eighteenth-century Presbyterian minister and abolitionist, presented a robust case for how it was possible to view the institution of slavery as unbiblical and unchristian. Bourne does not find a clear prohibition of slavery within Scripture, but he reasons within and from Scripture to make the following case:

The practice of slavery is not condemned in the Scriptures by that name, nor mentioned in any of our common law definitions by the same name. But it is condemned in the Scriptures under other names, and by descriptions, plainly and severely. There are many modern practices, such as piracy, dueling, gambling, &c., which are not condemned in Scriptures by those names, but by descriptions. In this way, though all the crimes against God and his religion have been legalised by men in this world, they are plainly described and condemned in the Scriptures, so that mankind are without any moral or just excuse for committing them. . . . Abundant additional evidence on the same doctrine [against slavery] is found in the fact, that the holding, exchanging, bartering, buying, selling and otherwise trading in human beings as property, and the licentiousness and prodigality, tyranny and cruelty produced by those practices are represented as among the greatest sins and threatened with the severest Divine judgments and punishments, in various other parts of the Scriptures, see Deut. xxviii. 68; 2 Chron. xxviii. 8–15; Neh. v. 5–15; Ps. xliv. 12; Isa. liii. 3–6; Jer. xv. 13–14; Ezek. xxvii. 2, 13, 26–36; Joel iii. 3–8; Amos ii. 6–7; Obad. 11; Nah. iii. 10; Zech. xi. 5; &c. According to the letter and spirit of these passages, such treatment of human beings is deserving of death, though in some of them the same treatment is threatened as the punishment of the greatest sins, which amounts to the same thing, because human slavery is the living death and destruction of its victims—while in most of the same passages public destruction or national death is threatened, as the Divine retaliatory punishment for the public or customary practice of the same treatment, as their context clearly shows.[5]

Christian doctrine has developed and will no doubt continue to do so in the future in some respects. As such, theological orthodoxy, by which I mean authentic and historical Christian faith, should not be identified with one particular moment of the church's confessional history. The church is always trying to preserve its commitment to Scripture while simultaneously seeking to discern how Scripture makes

5. George Bourne, *A Condensed Anti-Slavery Bible Argument: By a Citizen of Virginia* (New York: S. W. Benedict, 1845), 9, 18–19.

sense and works in our given context. Don't get me wrong, this is not a license to just make stuff up under the pretext of "development of doctrine." The history of heresy has shown that radical innovation, capitulation to culture, or attempts to modify Scripture are always injurious to the church's most holy faith. God doesn't give us new light, but God has new light to shed upon his word, as some of the Puritans said. As a result, it should be remembered that doctrinal development must be organic rather than alien, consistent with biblical logic, building on apostolic foundations, and pursuing consensus in the churches of the world. While theology concerns itself with the quest for what is right—right belief, right worship, and right practice—the church's verdict in its belief and ethics has always been provisional (what is right is open to correction) and contextual (rightness is sometimes a matter of circumstance).

THINKING FAITHFULLY AND CONSTRUCTIVELY ABOUT BIBLICAL AUTHORITY

In this chapter I've tried to explain that the real hallmark of a Christian view of Scripture is treating it as normative rather than negotiable. Even so, I've been brutally honest in pointing out the problems with a naïve view of living under biblical authority. We should avoid the extremes: on the one hand, brazenly taking a pair scissors to the parts of the Bible one doesn't care for (the progressive option) or, on the other hand, living and worshipping as if all commands in the Bible were equally relevant and equally applicable to us now (the hyperliteral option). There are some good reasons that we don't do some of the things the Bible commands, like stoning people for adultery, and why we do some things the Bible prohibits, like eating pork.

Scripture should not be read for the purpose of winning intellectual arguments but with an attitude of reverent obedience like that of the Psalmist: "I have hidden your word in my heart that I might not sin against you" (Psalm 119:11). Ezra is also a role model for he "devoted himself to the study and observance of the Law of the LORD, and to teaching its decrees and laws in Israel" (Ezra 7:10). We must seek to apply the word studied to our own situations.

—*Samuel Waje Kunhiyop*, African Christian Ethics *(Nairobi: Hippo, 2008), 50–51.*

Beyond the whole quagmire of normativity and authority, I encourage you to remember that God confronts us in Scripture with his demands for our obedience, not our half-hearted agreement to things that are momentarily convenient. If we love our Lord, then we must love his word and strive to obey it with all our heart, mind, strength, and soul. The difference between the followers and the fans, the sheep and the goats, true Christianity and consumerist religion, is that followers are those who promise to "listen and obey" (Deuteronomy 5:27), who hide God's word in their hearts (Psalm 119:11), who obey Jesus's teaching as an expression of their love for him (John 14:23–24), and who build their house on the foundation of Jesus's words (Matthew 7:24–26).

RECOMMENDED READING

Enns, Peter. *How the Bible Actually Works: In Which I Explain How an Ancient, Ambiguous, and Diverse Book Leads Us to Wisdom Rather Than Answers—and Why That's Great News.* New York: HarperOne, 2019.

Marshall, I. Howard. *Beyond the Bible: Moving from Scripture to Theology.* Grand Rapids: Baker, 2004.

Stott, John R. W. *Understanding the Bible.* Grand Rapids: Zondervan, 1999.

Witherington, Ben. *Reading and Understanding the Bible.* Oxford: Oxford University Press, 2014.

4

THE BIBLE IS *FOR* OUR TIME, BUT NOT *ABOUT* OUR TIME

The Bible is *for us*. It is the principal source for how to believe and behave as disciples of Jesus Christ. The Bible exists *for us* to have a God-centred view of creation, to understand God's providence in history, to hear God's promises, to know God's words of warning and encouragement, to have the words of Jesus, to hear the apostles' testimony about Jesus, and to look ahead to the kingdom in all its future fullness. The private and public reading of the Bible is *for us* in the sense that it is for our training, our edification, our transformation, and our encouragement. The Bible is *for us* since the Bible enables God to speak to people across the tide of history, through our manifold cultures and languages, and in a way that truly transcends human differences. Whether you are a second-century Christian in Rome, a fifth-century Arab Christian in the city of Tikrit, or a twenty-first-century believer in Zimbabwe, the Bible is God's word for you, for them, and for us today. The Bible is for us, yesterday, today, and until the end of the age.

However, **even though the Bible is _for us_, it was not written _to us_, nor was it written _about us_.** When we read the Bible, we are entering into a historically and culturally distant world and we must "mind the gap" as they say on the London Tube. In the rush to make the Bible instantaneously relevant, we can inadvertently misuse it by not recognizing the specific situation of the authors and lazily pick up something that seems handy to us on a first read. In terms of Bible study, this is like browsing Wikipedia rather than spending a few hours in your local library. Reading Scripture for quick practical application, and ignoring the social, historical, and cultural gap, is like looking for instant gratification without the hard labor of study.

The problem is that if we _disrespect_ the historical distance, we will potentially _distort_ the Bible's proper interpretation. Accordingly, it is essential to ask what Isaiah 53 meant for the Judean exiles in sixth-century Babylon before we ask how it applies to twenty-first-century Baltimore, Brisbane, or Bogotá. I know this is going to sound strange, but in order to make the Bible meaningful, relevant, and applicable, the Bible first must be defamiliarized and dislocated from our own time.[1] In other words, we have to grasp how strange the biblical world is before we can try to

---

1. Religious historian Jonathan Z. Smith (_Imagining Religion: From Babylon to Jonestown_ [Chicago: University of Chicago Press, 1982], xiii) noted how beneficial it was in "making the familiar seem strange in order to enhance our perception of the familiar."

make it familiar to our own audiences, or to say that again, we have to realize how different the Bible is from our own time before we can allow it to speak to our own contemporary situation. Otherwise, we will end up with a superficial reading of the Bible, or worse, we will end up reading our own context and times into the Bible.

There is a real danger that we become overly familiar with the Bible in the sense that we read our own experiences into it. We have to remember that the biblical world was rather unlike our place and time. People who work in biblical translation deal with this problem all the time. I mean, just how much of the Bible can you translate into a culture, and how much do you have to leave untranslated? When Bible translators first came to Papua New Guinea, they had a problem. How do you say that Jesus is the "Lamb of God who takes away the sins of the world" to people who have never seen a lamb and who have no idea what a lamb looks like or how lambs were used for sacrifices and meat in the Middle East? Now, in Papua New Guinea they do have pigs, which were symbols of prosperity and wealth, and pigs were used in indigenous religious practices. So could you say that "Jesus is the Pig of God who takes away the sins of the world"? Perhaps, but probably not a good idea given Old Testament prohibitions on consuming pork, which would create confusion. So probably best to leave it as "Lamb," and then when someone asks, "What is a lamb?" go ahead and explain it to them. But I hope you get the point. Some things need to be left untranslated, kept different, and made foreign in order to properly understand them.

The problem is that in the psychology of reading we cannot help but associate the familiar with the unfamiliar, in the hope of understanding better. We always associate the words, images, and metaphors in a text with our own experience of those same words, images, and metaphors. While the commonality of human experience is what makes translation and reading possible, there is the danger of projecting your own experience of something, whether lambs or temples, into the text you are reading. The problem is that things we take for granted, think of as self-evident, or plainly assume, were often quite different to ancient peoples. When Isaiah or Luke mentions X, we might assume that X meant to them the same thing it means to us. But this is frequently not the case. Often words, concepts, and symbols had different meanings in the ancient world than in our modern world. Let me demonstrate that to you by showing how the words "religion," "gift," and "hospitality" meant very different things in the ancient world than what they do now.

HOW A LITTLE BACKGROUND KNOWLEDGE CAN BRING BIG INSIGHTS

When Religion Is Not Actually Religious

Those of us living in the modern West tend to think of "religion" as the sphere of the sacred, to do with beliefs about God, with ethical obligations commanded by God, and connected to virtues like charity. Moreover, religion for us is distinct from the secular world with its neutral public places and institutions like government and education. However, in the ancient world, "religion" was not about beliefs and ethics; rather, it was about duties to the gods largely in terms of rituals. The ancient world also had no secularism with the separation of church and state; instead, things like religion, government, economics, business, citizenship, ethnicity, and military commands were all bound tightly together. Accordingly, when Paul commends the Athenians for being "religious," they are not thinking that Paul likes their theology and ethics, which are separate from their politics; no, they are thinking of Paul as affirming the way that they perform their duties to honor the gods in sacrifices, prayers, and other rituals (Acts 17:22).[2]

When Gift-Giving Is Not Free

We tend to associate gift-giving with entirely gratuitous generosity with the expectation of nothing in return, yet that was not ordinarily what gift-giving meant in the ancient world. In the ancient world, gifts usually had some reciprocal expectation, strings attached, some indebtedness making it incumbent upon the recipient to return some favour or service to the gift-giver. All gifts had an implicit quid pro quo, even if there was a measure of generosity shown by one side. One thing that is striking about the apostle Paul's theology of grace is that his notion of the divine gift of salvation

---

2. The best study on this is by Brent Nongbri, *Before Religion: A History of a Modern Concept* (New Haven, CT: Yale University Press, 2015); for a shorter and more accessible explanation see Michael F. Bird and N. T. Wright, *The New Testament in Its World* (Grand Rapids: Zondervan Academic, 2019), 152–58.

is not about reciprocity but incongruity: God bestows his gift of grace in a way that people can never fully pay him back (see Romans 5:15–17; 6:23). Knowing a little bit about ancient gift-giving helps show us how Paul's theology of grace and divine gifts stands out.[3]

When Hospitality Is Way beyond Friends

People today tend to think of hospitality as something they do for friends and relatives—having them over for a meal or taking them out for dinner. But in the ancient world, hospitality is what one did for strangers, people they did not know or did not know if they could fully trust (see Romans 12:13; 1 Timothy 5:10; Hebrews 13:2; 3 John 8)![4]

God invites and demands that God's people be a people of hospitality. So what's at stake? A church or individual that does not practice hospitality misunderstands the identity of the Triune God and, as a result, the very meaning of Christian identity and life.

—*Joshua Jipp**

* Tavis Bohlinger, "Does Biblical Hospitality Mean Martha Stewart? Joshua Jipp Says No," *The Lab*, September 29, 2018, https://academic.logos.com/does-biblical -hospitality-mean-martha-stewart-joshua-jipp-says-no/.

---

3. This was recently demonstrated by John Barclay, *Paul and the Gift* (Grand Rapids: Eerdmans, 2015).

4. As shown ably by Joshua W. Jipp, *Saved by Faith and Hospitality* (Grand Rapids: Eerdmans, 2017).

Moving from Familiarity, to Strangeness, to Application

So if we think that the ancient world divided religion from politics or thought of religion in terms of beliefs and ethics, then we will misunderstand references to "religion" in places like the book of Acts (Acts 17:22; 25:19; 26:5). Or if we read our own idea of "gift" back into Romans 5:15–17 and 6:23, we will likely miss something or misunderstand the radical nature of Paul's point about how lavish God's grace is toward us. Likewise, if we think "hospitality" just means hanging out with our nice middle-class church friends, we will not actually be obeying the command "Do not forget to show hospitality to strangers" (Hebrews 13:2). We will not be engaging in biblical hospitality which requires looking after the immigrant, the stranger, and the refugee in our midst.

Therefore, in order to understand the Bible, you have to "defamiliarize" or "other" the Bible. To be clear, I do not mean treating the Bible as a historical relic with little or no relevance for our own day. I am not suggesting we study the historical context of the Bible solely for the purpose of creating a museum of funny old words and strange ideas to be analysed for curiosity's sake. Rather, I mean studying the Bible afresh, recognizing its distinctive location and purpose, grasping its situatedness and its own back-then-ness. Once the Bible seems strange to us, then we can reread it anew, on its own terms, without projecting ourselves or our own culture into it. Thereafter, we are enabled and encouraged to find new, exciting, and challenging ways to make it relevant for us.

Therefore, the aim of this chapter is to highlight the importance of knowing historical background, entering the world and culture of antiquity, and the big payoffs you get in understanding and applying the Bible if you labor just a little in historical context.

BETTER KNOWLEDGE OF BACKGROUND MAKES FOR BETTER APPLICATION

There are several well-known texts that I think show the value of knowing some background about the world around the Bible in order to have a better grasp of the Bible.

The Image of God

Then God said, "Let us make mankind in our *image*, in our *likeness*, so that they may rule over the fish in the sea and the birds in the sky, over the livestock and all the wild animals, and over all the creatures that move along the ground."

So God created mankind in his own *image*,
in the *image of God* he created them;
male and female he created them.
(Genesis 1:26–27)

This is one of the most famous texts in the Christian Bible. It is so important for our doctrine of humanity—the belief that every person, male and female, bears the *imago dei* or the image of God. But what precisely is the "image" in the "image of God"?

The image of God has normally been identified with a particular trait or ability that humans possess: something along the lines of the capacity for reasoning and reflection, the ability to engage in rational discourse, a mixture of self-awareness and God-awareness, our disposition to form relationships, the ability to be driven by more than instinct and base desire, a desire to know and be known. In other words, the image of God is usually associated with *human* rationality and relationality.

I have to confess that defining the image as either a rational ability or a relational capacity has always bugged me. It could imply that people who are cognitively impaired (Down Syndrome or dementia) or relationally challenged (autism or Asperger's) are somehow diminished or dispossessed of the image of God. However, it stopped bugging me when I learned some Old Testament background about the meaning of the image of God in the context of the ancient Near East.

In the course of my studies, I learned that in parts of the ancient Near East the "image of god" was an exalted title for monarchs.[5] Kings were regarded as special servants of the gods and accordingly bore their image as rulers of the earth. In the New Kingdom of Egypt (1500s BC), the Egyptian pharaoh is lauded as the "image of Re" and "image of Atum." The Assyrian king Esarhaddon was addressed as the "image of Bel" and "image of Marduk" (600s BC). In a

---

5. David J. A. Clines, "The Image of God in Man," *Tyndale Bulletin* 19 (1968): 53–103; Walter Brueggemann, "From Dust to Kingship," *Zeitschrift für die alttestamentlich Wissenschaft* 84 (1972): 1–18.

papyrus fragment from Egypt during the Ptolemaic period (200s BC), we find a reference to the monarch as "a living image of Zeus, son of the Sun."[6] The Greek philosopher Plutarch (AD 100) said, "Now justice is the aim and end of law, but law is the work of the ruler, and the ruler is the image of God who orders all things."[7]

What this means is that rather than regard the "image of God" as a rational ability or relational capacity, if we take into account the ancient Near Eastern context, then Genesis 1:26–27 is saying that all of humanity is royal in God's eyes. The image is not an aptitude or ability; it is a status, something given to all humans irrespective of gender, ethnicity, or ableness. Whereas the image was restricted to an elite few monarchs who were worshipped as godlike figures, the privilege of bearing God's image is democratized in the biblical narrative so that all humanity shares in it.[8] Humanity is thus royal in God's sight and is given the important task of ruling and stewarding creation as God's vice-regent. On this perspective, God is a generous Creator who shares power with his creatures by inviting them and trusting them to participate in his reign over the world.[9]

The upshot of all this is that knowing the ancient Near

---

6. S. R. Llewelyn, ed., *New Documents Illustrating Early Christianity*, vol. 9 (Grand Rapids: Eerdmans, 2002), 36.

7. Plutarch, *To an Uneducated Ruler* 780e5–f2, cited in Sean McDonough, *Christ as Creator: The Origins of a New Testament Doctrine* (New York: Oxford University Press, 2009), 58.

8. Victor P. Hamilton, *The Book of Genesis*, New International Commentary on the Old Testament (Grand Rapids: Eerdmans, 1990), 135.

9. J. Richard Middleton, *The Liberating Image: The Imago Dei in Genesis 1* (Grand Rapids: Brazos, 2005), 296–97.

Eastern background of the "image of God" inoculates us against thinking it is about human capacity or ability, something which would diminish the cognitively impaired or the socially challenged as God's image bearers. Rather, the image of God means that humans are divinely royal, the cosmic billboards for expressing God's sovereignty and presence in the world, and that all people possess the image and participate in the vocation to radiate God's majesty in the world.

Paying Taxes to Caesar

Later they sent some of the Pharisees and Herodians to Jesus to catch him in his words. They came to him and said, "Teacher, we know that you are a man of integrity. You aren't swayed by others, because you pay no attention to who they are; but you teach the way of God in accordance with the truth. Is it right to pay the imperial tax to Caesar or not? Should we pay or shouldn't we?"

But Jesus knew their hypocrisy. "Why are you trying to trap me?" he asked. "Bring me a denarius and let me look at it." They brought the coin, and he asked them, "Whose image is this? And whose inscription?"

"Caesar's," they replied.

Then Jesus said to them, "Give back to Caesar what is Caesar's and to God what is God's."

And they were amazed at him. (Mark 12:13–17)

I've heard several sermons on this passage and the application is always predictably the same. It usually runs along the lines of paying taxes to Caesar, Uncle Sam, or whoever it is that runs the government. Christians should pay taxes and be honest in our fiscal dealings with the government; but remember, the church belongs to God, not to the government. So pay your taxes and try to keep church and state separate. That application would be fine if the text we were looking at was something like Romans 13:1–7 about paying taxes or 1 Peter 2:13–17 about obeying and respecting the emperor. The problem is, however, this story is not about that.

For a start, what you need to know is that the story is not recounting how the Pharisees and Herodians posed a legitimate question about taxation to Jesus because they were really stumped about whether or not paying taxes was a good idea and they really wanted to know what Jesus thought about the matter. This story is not about taxes; the whole thing was a trap designed to catch Jesus and get him in big trouble with the imperial authorities. How did the trap work? Well, this is where some background is very useful, even necessary. If you read the Jewish historian Josephus, you'll discover that a group of rather zealous Galileans, those anxious to throw off the yoke of Roman oppression by means of violent revolution, had a motto, "No king but God." And since paying taxes to Caesar meant recognizing him as king, paying taxes meant recognizing Caesar as king instead of Israel's God, insinuating that the payment of taxes to Caesar was both a blasphemous and cowardly betrayal of God's unique authority over Israel.[10] So when Jesus was

---

10. See Josephus, *Antiquities* 18.23; *Wars* 2.118; 7.410.

asked about paying taxes to Caesar, he was put in a catch-22. If he said, "Yes, pay them," then Jesus would look like he either had compromised God's sovereignty or else was cowering in fear to the Romans. Alternatively, if Jesus said, "No, don't pay them," then the Herodians could have had Jesus arrested on the spot under charges of sedition for forbidding the payment of taxes which was an offence—precisely the claim they fabricated against Jesus at his trial (Luke 23:2). To quote Admiral Ackbar, "It's a trap!"

In addition, you need to know how Jesus's response rode on the inscription on the coin. Notice Jesus's response: he didn't try to bluff his way through an answer. Instead, he requested a denarius and asked, "Whose image and inscription are on it?" Now, various coins were minted in Judea, mostly without imperial images, usually with floral designs (only Pontius Pilate printed coins depicting pagan cultic utensils, because he was a dude in a toga who wanted to see how much he could rile up the Jews). But this denarius was probably a Tiberian tribute penny which had on one side an "image" of Tiberius's face with an inscription that read, "Caesar Augustus Tiberius, Son of the Divine Augustus." Then, on the other side, it said, "High Priest," accompanied by a depiction of Tiberius's mother, Livia, posing as the goddess Roma, the patroness of Rome itself. What's that got to do with anything? Well, Jesus's point was that if Caesar was "divine," and if this was his "image," then it was a violation of the second commandment, which explicitly forbids making graven images of a god (see Exodus 20:4; Deuteronomy 5:8). Jesus was saying in effect, "You guys are carrying around pagan money which is an affront to our religion, so give the pagan king back his pagan money." Jesus turned the trap back on his questioners. They were the traitors to Israel's monotheistic worship, and they transgressed God's law by possessing such currency.

Lastly, there is even more to it—arguably, a dig at Caesar himself! Perhaps Jesus was saying that Caesar should have received taxes because he should have gotten *everything* that he deserved, and he meant everything! Much like how Judas Maccabeus, who led an uprising against the Syrians in the second century BC, urged his fellow Judeans to "pay back the gentiles in full," by which he meant violent retribution (1 Maccabees 2:68). Thus, far from acquiescing to the view that Jews should pay taxes, Jesus was being subversive, affirming a critique of pagan power over Israel, and avoiding the trap set for him.[11]

This is a great story about how Jesus wiped the floor with the Pharisees and Herodians, but in order to understand it, you need to know a bit about Galilean revolutionary movements, ancient Roman coinage, and a Maccabean battle cry.

D. A. Carson gives another good example of how knowing some basic archaeological information can prevent errors and wrongful interpretation of Scripture. Concerning Revelation 3:15–16, about the exalted Jesus's words to the Laodiceans, and his wanting to spit them out because they are neither hot nor cold, Carson writes:

---

11. See N. T. Wright, *Jesus and the Victory of God* (London: SPCK, 1996), 502–7.

A fair bit of nonsense has been written about the exalted Christ's words to the Laodiceans: "I know your deeds, that you are neither cold nor hot. I wish you were either one or the other!" (Rev 3:15). Many have argued that this means God prefers people who are "spiritually cold" above those who are "spiritually lukewarm," even though his first preference is for those who are "spiritually hot." Ingenious explanations are then offered to defend the proposition that spiritual coldness is a superior state to spiritual lukewarmness. All of this can comfortably be abandoned once responsible archaeology has made its contribution. Laodicea shared the Lycus valley with two other cities mentioned in the NT. Colossae was the only one that enjoyed fresh, cold, spring water; Hierapolis was known for its hot springs and became a place to which people would resort to enjoy these healing baths. By contrast, Laodicea put up with water that was neither cold and useful, nor hot and useful; it was lukewarm, loaded with chemicals, and with an international reputation for being nauseating. That brings us to Jesus' assessment of the Christians there: they were not useful in any sense, they were simply disgusting, so nauseating he would vomit them away. The interpretation would be clear enough to anyone living in the Lycus valley in the first century; it takes a bit of background information to make the point clear today.[12]

---

12. D. A. Carson, "Approaching the Bible," in *New Bible Commentary: 21st Century Edition*, ed. D. A. Carson, R. T. France, J. A. Motyer, and G. J. Wenham, 4th ed. (Downers Grove, IL: InterVarsity Press, 1994), 15–16.

A PRIESTHOOD OF SCHOLARS?

Some of my readers here may object that all this focus on historical background, cultural context, and ancient environment as necessary for understanding the Bible means that the Bible will end up belonging to a few elite historians who alone have the expertise to read and understand all this stuff. *What chance do we laypeople have for understanding the Bible if we don't read Akkadian, Ugaritic, Hebrew, Aramaic, Greek, Latin, or Coptic texts in their original languages? How can we competently explain the Bible to our friends and family if we haven't read the Babylonian creation epics, the Dead Sea Scrolls, the complete writings of Philo or philosophers like Cicero or Seneca, or kept up with the latest archaeological reports out of Galilee or Ephesus?* I am guessing you might feel very intimidated by all this knowledge out there—knowledge that you don't have and don't have the time or skills to even begin acquiring.

Is All This Focus on Historical Background Elitist?

Some of you may go so far as to say that this focus on historical background is not only daunting but dangerous, because it means that a "priesthood of scholars" will effectively become a council of self-appointed judges who determine biblical interpretation based on their own hyper-specialized areas of expertise.[13] Even worse, so it goes, some of

---

13. Such a complaint is lodged by Guy Waters, *Justification and the New Perspective on Paul: A Review and a Response* (Phillipsburg, NJ: P&R, 2004), 154–56, 193, and Wayne Grudem, "The Perspicuity of Scripture," *Themelios* 34 (2009): 297.

these so-called experts we rely on are not Christians—some are even flat-out unbelievers who try to disprove the Bible—so who would trust them over a godly layperson's account of biblical interpretation? Plus, these "experts" are hardly of one mind on anything, and they continually argue among themselves over the minutiae of facts and figures. On top of that, the emergence of new evidence or new theories is constantly leading them to revise their understanding of things like the reign of King David or Paul's ministry in Corinth.

You might retort that you believe in the priesthood of all believers, whereas I am advocating a magisterium of godless professors who get all uppity and presume to lecture you on the Bible while disbelieving it themselves. You might prefer to believe that every soul is competent to interpret the Bible for himself or herself, and you don't need some pompous professors acting like self-appointed bishops, telling you what to believe or how to pray or preach, based on some new Aramaic word that's been discovered or a pottery sherd that's just been dug up in Egypt. "No thanks," you might reply, "I'm good. No history for me!"

Like It or Not, Biblical Study Requires Historical Study

If that is you, take a deep breath and stay with me for a moment. Look, if you pick up the Bible and read from Genesis to Revelation, sure, you can get a pretty good grasp of the basic storyline of God. If you read the Bible attentively, you can figure out the basic storyline of creation, the fall, the patriarchs, Israel, Jesus, the church, and the end of all things. You can get a basic grip on the Bible without learning ancient Aramaic, earning a PhD in Egyptology, or going on a summer excavation of Pergamum in modern Turkey. You could also attain a basic idea of who God is, who Jesus is, what the church is about, what the gospel is, and grasp the fundamentals of discipleship. A rudimentary understanding of the Bible can be attained through a close and careful reading of it, being attentive to how the Bible's storyline progresses and noting how the Bible effectively interprets itself. Besides, we have the illuminating work of the Holy Spirit, through whom God brings understanding to our minds so we can grasp and apply all that God says to us in Scripture. Thus, a basic and sufficient understanding of the Bible can be attained without earning a PhD in Second Temple Jewish literature.

However, if you read the Bible from scratch, and if you are a bit of a novice at reading it, the fact is that you are going to have huge questions that you will not be able to answer. Just where is "Shittim" and who are the "Moabites" (Numbers 25:1), what is the difference between "Israel" and "Judea" during the period of the divided monarchy (1 Kings 12:20–21), what happened in between Malachi and Matthew (some four hundred years!), who were the "Herodians" (Mark 3:6), and just which presidential nominee am I supposed to identify as the "Mother of Prostitutes" (Revelation 17:5)? That is precisely why study Bibles are so popular and so important: they have notes that explain all that technical stuff that you have no idea where to even begin looking up.

On top of that, if you are reading the Bible alone, that's great, but you should also be reading the Bible as part of a community, with your church, with a group of friends, or even as a family. There you will encounter people who have been reading the Bible longer than you have, and you will pick up a few things that they've learned about background and context. Yes, while Protestants don't like having to rely on a professor or pope to tell them what to believe, and they generally affirm the clarity of Scripture, they also know that clarity is not evenly distributed across the Bible. This is why the Westminster Confession of Faith (1649) and the London Baptist Confession (1689) state:

> All things in Scripture are not alike plain in themselves, nor alike clear unto all: yet those things which are necessary to be known, believed, and observed for salvation are so clearly propounded, and opened in some place of Scripture or other, that not only the learned, but the unlearned, in a due use of the ordinary means, may attain unto a sufficient understanding of them.[14]

So, yeah, figuring out how to get right with God from reading the Bible is pretty straightforward, but after that, you might need one of those nerd guys and gals called "teachers" or "pastors" to help you understand things. Then, in extremely rare and technical cases, maybe you even need a biblical scholar, philologist, or archaeologist to help too. From time to time, we all need a Philip to run beside our chariot to answer our questions about what we are reading in Scripture (Acts 8:26–36). In addition, I would not deny the illuminating work of the Spirit in assisting Christians

---

14. WCF 1.7; LBC 1.7.

in gaining a basic and adequate understanding of the Bible. However, by immersing ourselves in the culture, texts, and artefacts of the ancient world, we give the Holy Spirit more to work with in terms of opening our minds and hearts to the core issues that the biblical authors were talking about.

D. A. Carson on why we need to know historical background:

God has disclosed himself to us in Scripture, in particular people, in particular language, in particular space-time history—it is a historical revelation. And so even when you do your philology, when you are doing your word studies, you are asking what those words meant at the time, you are asking how the Greek syntax works. But when they [the Bible authors] use [certain] expressions, when you have a veil over somebody's face, or when a woman comes in and washes Jesus's feet with her hair when he's at table, somebody has got to explain that somewhere.[15]

MY BEST TIP: READ ANCIENT STUFF

If I may shock you with a rhetorical point—and maybe I should—I would go so far as to say that anyone who only knows the Bible, and not the wider history of antiquity, does not really know the Bible. To know the Bible is to know its

---

15. Quoted in Jonathan Parnell, "Serving to Master Two?–Historical Background and the Bible," *Desiring God*, July 27, 2011, www.desiringgod.org /articles/serving-to-master-two-historical-background-and-the-bible.

world, because meaning is determined by context, and context is what saves us from grave errors of interpretation. So rather than read popular trade books like *Help! I'm Trapped in a Christian Prairie Romance Novel*, or *Ten Biblical Tax Shelters*, or *40 Days of Your Best Life to the Prayer of Jabez's Shack Code*, immerse yourself instead in the literature of the ancient world.

HOW TO BEGIN LEARNING ABOUT BIBLE BACKGROUND: A SAMPLER

- Listen to *The Lost World of Genesis One* by John Walton (InterVarsity Press) as an audio book.
- Watch "Historical Setting of Isaiah" by Andrew Abernethy (Ridley College) on YouTube.
- Listen to Donald Kagan's "Introduction to Ancient Greek History," Yale University podcast.
- Read 1–2 Maccabees in the Common English Bible.
- Watch "Encountering the Holy Land" on Zondervan's MasterLectures streaming service.
- Read 1 Enoch 37–71 from the *Old Testament Pseudepigrapha*, edited by James Charlesworth.
- Listen to Gary Rendsburg's "The Dead Sea Scrolls" (Audible) audio book.
- Watch *The New Testament You Never Knew* DVD or download from Zondervan.
- Read Josephus's *War of the Jews* in the Loeb Classical Library.
- Read the *Epistle to Diognetus* in a translation by either Michael Holmes or Rick Brannan.

To get more out of your Bible reading you don't need to have a PhD in ancient literature and religion; you only need to begin reading ancient works in English in order to reap some of the benefits of having a better knowledge of biblical backgrounds. To twist a famous quote from a certain character from a certain TV show: "I read and then I know things!" So if you want to know the Bible better, read more history *about* the ancient world and especially history *from* the ancient world. My advice is that you become a wide-ranging reader who includes regular readings from the ancient world in your reading diet.

Read some Josephus, the Dead Sea Scrolls, the Apocrypha, the histories of Tacitus, the apostolic fathers. Or subscribe to a Bible and archaeology magazine. Watch some YouTube videos about the Persians and Greeks. Find a good podcast or streaming service about the Bible in its world. Get a decent study Bible on history and archaeology. Consult some reference works on Bible backgrounds. These things are what will enhance the depth and sophistication of your reading of Scripture and yield exegetical insights, theological transformation, and perhaps even spiritual blessings.

The eminent scholar of ancient Judaism and Christianity, James H. Charlesworth, once said that he inherited several libraries from Christian scholars and pastors who had passed away and in every one of them was a copy of William Whiston's translation of the *Complete Works of Josephus*.[16] Our forefathers in the faith knew the value of using the

---

16. James Charlesworth, *Jesus within Judaism: New Light from Exciting Archaeological Discoveries* (New York: Doubleday, 1989), 90.

historical sources of the apostolic era in their study of the word of God—as should we. This will improve your Bible reading immediately, which in turn will shape your theology, discipleship, and ministry.

RECOMMENDED READING

Arnold, Clinton. *Zondervan Illustrated Bible Backgrounds Commentary.* 5 vols. Grand Rapids: Zondervan, 2016.

Beers, Holly. *A Week in the Life of a Greco-Roman Woman.* Downers Grove, IL: InterVarsity Press, 2019.

Bock, Darrell L., and Gregory J. Herrick. *Jesus in Context: Background Readings for Gospel Study.* Grand Rapids: Baker, 2005.

Dodson, Derek, and Katherine E. Smith. *Exploring Biblical Backgrounds: A Reader in History and Literary Contexts.* Waco, TX: Baylor University Press, 2018.

Evans, Craig A., and Stanley E. Porter, eds. *Dictionary of New Testament Background.* Downers Grove, IL: InterVarsity Press, 2000.

Keener, Craig S. *The IVP Bible Background Commentary: New Testament.* Downers Grove, IL: InterVarsity Press, 2014.

Walton, John H., Victor H. Matthews, and Mark Chavalas. *The IVP Bible Background Commentary.* Downers Grove, IL: InterVarsity Press, 2000.

5

WE SHOULD TAKE THE BIBLE SERIOUSLY, BUT NOT ALWAYS LITERALLY

I ordinarily refrain from correcting people's English. However, I draw the line at the word "literally." I care not how many friends I lose, how many awkward looks I receive, or whether my students perceive me as condescending and pedantic. I must stop people from using the word "literally" in a literally wrong way.

Because of the overuse and wrongful use of the word "literally," it is now given two meanings in most dictionaries: (a) in a literal manner or sense; exactly; and (b) used for emphasis while not being literally true.

For example, maybe you have witnessed or even participated in conversations that run something like this:

> "I died, I literally died!" he said with both hands raised emphatically, speaking to a group of us about a very embarrassing incident.
>
> "No, no, you didn't 'literally' die," I woodenly replied. "If you had died, you wouldn't be here to tell us about it in such a melodramatic fashion, would you now?"
>
> "Gosh, Mike, great way to kill a cool story," he retorted while everyone else rolled their eyes at me.

Sadly, when it comes to the meaning of "literally," I am fighting a losing battle. That is because according to many dictionaries these days, the word "literally" has been adjusted and broadened to reflect popular usage among people. In other words, the incorrect usage of the word "literally" has literally been added to the dictionary. The word "literally" now means (1) something true in a literal manner or exact sense; or (2) a form of emphasis even if not literally true. Ugh! It's like the English dictionary committees have been taken over by illiterate marauders committed to pillaging the English language of all its sensibilities and manners . . . or possibly by American teenagers who offer the English language the same degree of respect as Viking raiders showed to the Scottish Hebrides.

What does this tidbit of information have to do with the Bible? Well, many good Christian folks pride themselves on taking the Bible literally, and they mean literally in the proper sense of "literally"—true to the word and letter. A commitment to so-called biblical literalism is intended as an antidote against so-called liberal interpretations of biblical texts. However, I can assure you that no one—neither the pulpit-pounding fundamentalist nor the doggedly doctrinaire conservative—interprets the Bible in an unwavering, consistent, and strictly literal manner. You can't. It is impossible to do so, unless you entertain manifold absurdities. Let me prove it to you, as I recount a fairly typical interaction I have with seminary students from time to time:

"I take the Bible literally," a bearded, bespectacled twenty-something young man proudly confessed to me.

"Mmm, no you don't!" I replied.

"Ahem, yes I do, thank you!"

"Well, when Jesus says, 'I am the door' (John 10:9), and 'I am the true vine' (John 15:1), do you think that Jesus is *literally* a six-foot wooden door made of mahogany or *literally* a tangled vine on the side of a hill full of juicy red grapes?"

"No, of course not, that's just stupid. I mean the Bible should normally be interpreted in a literal grammatico-historical and plain commonsense fashion."

"Grammatico-historical? Normally? Really? I'm not so sure, bro! For example, when the apostle Paul says 'these things'—by which he means Genesis 16–21 with the story of Abraham, Sarah, Hagar, and their sons Jacob and Ishmael—should be taken 'allegorically,' are you suggesting that Paul was wrong and we should deliberately read against his own apostolic reading strategy? Or what about 1 Corinthians 9:9–10 when Paul explains Deuteronomy 25:4 about not muzzling an ox while it is treading out the grain and he applies it in a spiritual or social sense of sharing what material resources we have with others? Would you chide Paul for his spiritualized and socialist interpretation of Mosaic legislation about animal husbandry?"

The young man paused long, his mind ticking over, thinking of a comeback or counterexample. Before he did, I added, "And don't even get me started on interpreting the book of Revelation literally. In one place, John told us that his book should be taken *spiritually*, at least in relation to Jerusalem where the two witnesses die, because in John's vision the city of Jerusalem came to represent and rehearse the idolatry and rebellion of ancient Sodom and Egypt (Revelation 11:8). And did John think that Jesus really has the words 'KING OF KINGS AND LORD OF LORDS' tattooed on his leg (Revelation 19:16) and a flying sword that comes out of his mouth (19:15, 21)? I don't think so. And then we could get into Jesus's parables, or the Song of Songs, or the imprecatory psalms."

TAKING THE BIBLE SERIOUSLY IS NOT ALWAYS TAKING THE BIBLE LITERALLY

No one, and I mean no one, can offer a consistently literal interpretation of the Bible. For me, this issue of taking the

Bible literally, while often treated as a mark of conservatism, is simply a red herring and a pointless distraction from the real struggle to discern God's will in Holy Scripture. **The real issue is not whether we take the Bible *literally*, but whether we take the Bible *seriously*.** Are we serious about its language, its historical contexts, its genres, its complexities, the problems it throws up at us, its inspiring power, its beauty, the strenuous nature of its commands, its historical distance and cultural weirdness, its storyline, how the New Testament uses the Old, how the church has understood it through the centuries, and how to live obediently under its promises? That is what matters, not a commitment to some kind of interpretive gold standard called biblical literalism. Christian faith does not require biblical literalism; rather, it requires serious and sober-minded effort to wrestle with its weight—often more than we can bear! Which is why we study the Bible as part of a community, a community around us with teachers and pastors, a community with members who have already entered the heavenly Jerusalem ahead of us, and whose collective wisdom is our inheritance.

In what follows, I'm going to explain how to take the Bible seriously, not through strict literalism but by understanding "meaning," and provide some tips for interpretation.

THE MATTER OF MEANING AND THE MEANING OF THE MATTER

Have you ever had a discussion or disagreement with someone over the meaning of a biblical text? You've probably heard statements like "I think what John means is . . ."

or "What it means to me is . . ." or "No, I don't think that's what it means." However, let's back up for a second and ask a more basic question. What is "meaning"? When we say a text "means" something, what are we saying? When we talk about "meaning," what do we "literally" mean by that? How does meaning happen? Where is meaning to be found?

Two Types of Understanding

I think it helps if we distinguish interpretation as **literary understanding** from interpretation as **significance and application**.

First, when you read something like "when Jesus had entered Capernaum, a centurion came to him, asking for help," you comprehend or understand that the text is telling you that Jesus entered a Galilean village called Capernaum and while in the vicinity of Capernaum a centurion came and asked Jesus for his assistance (Matthew 8:5). In your head, you unconsciously analyse, describe, and paraphrase the information presented to you in a biblical text. That way you can repeat the information when asked. That is interpretation as basic comprehension of the text.

Second, beyond literary comprehension, there is also a type of understanding that has to do with significance, that is to say, thinking through a text's implications and the various ways it can resonate with you. Here, understanding goes beyond grasping basic information and is a kind of association you make, consciously or not, between a biblical text and other things you have in your own mental encyclopedia. We are asking, what does this verse, this passage, this chapter, or this book remind me of, make me think about, and relate to? You see, meaning is the web of connections that we make between a text, other texts, and our experiences in the world. The meaning of a text is really just all of the related information that lights up inside your head as you read a text. What a text means to you is basically what is happening inside your mind when you try to put the text into relationship with what you already know. How does the information in the text relate to what you already believe and intuitively know? What is more, the information acquired from reading a text is then added to your overall pool of literary knowledge and cognitively filed away until a later experience requires you to recall it.

For example, when I read the parable of the wicked tenants in Mark 12:1–12, several things jump to my mind:

- The parable is also found in different versions in Matthew, Luke, and even the Gospel of Thomas §65.
- The parable seems to rehearse Isaiah 5 where Israel is the vineyard and God is the vineyard owner.
- The parable functions as another prediction of Jesus's passion much like Mark 8:31; 9:12, 31; and 10:33–34.
- The son who is seized, killed, and thrown out of the vineyard obviously represents Jesus, and the wicked tenants are the Jerusalem leadership.
- The punch line is verse 9 with the words, "What then will the owner of the vineyard do? He will come and kill those tenants and give the vineyard to others," which makes the parable an oracle of judgment against the chief priests, the teachers of the law, and the elders.

- Most of the parables that Jesus told in the Gospel of Mark are in the context of conflict with his socio-religious rivals.
- Psalm 118, cited at the end of the parable, is one of the most quoted psalms in the whole New Testament.
- This would be a hard text to preach because the application does not automatically jump out at you. Perhaps I would make the big idea, "Don't be a wicked tenant," or perhaps, "Enjoy the vineyard that God has given to you."
- I think I saw someone do a good children's talk on this passage, or its parallel from Matthew, on YouTube.

And that, at first blush, is what Mark 12:1–12 and the parable of the wicked tenants means to me. However, that is obviously not all it can mean and all it does mean. Other people—past, present, and future—can detect other resonances, connotations, and applications beyond what I've said.

The Trinity of Meaning: Authors, Texts, and Readers

So "meaning" is how, at one level, we grasp the basic story inside a text or the features of an argument that a text lays out. But at another level, meaning is what I remember and think about when I read a text. However, if I may ratchet up the intensity a bit, biblical interpreters go beyond this and are concerned with the precise place of meaning in a biblical text. Where does biblical meaning come from? A few different options present themselves to us. Those are the author, the text, and the reader! Is meaning about figuring out any one of these, a combination of them, or some other path toward discerning how texts give and receive meaning by interpreters?

Author's Intention?

For some people, meaning is the same thing as **authorial intent**. So, once we have figured out what an author was trying to say to his or her audience, then we know what a text means. The task of the reader is to decipher from a text what an author intended to say, and that is the sum of all meaning. Simple! Well, not quite. Two problems present themselves.

First, what God or even a human author meant to communicate in a biblical text is not always clear to us. It is not like God gave us an answer key at the end of the Bible or we can interview the author to check and see if we got the main point. Authors are not always clear as to what they are talking about. For instance, what does Paul mean when he says, "For if a woman does not cover her head, she might as well have her hair cut off; but if it is a disgrace for a woman to have her hair cut off or her head shaved, then she should cover her head" (1 Corinthians 11:6)? I have a few ideas, but I do not have certainty, and I don't think anyone can be certain of Paul's intention here.

Second, authors can sometimes be wiser than they know, and their words can often take on a meaning beyond what they intended. Consider this: Did the prophet Isaiah think that the Suffering Servant (described in Isaiah 53) referred to Israel, to himself, to some unspecified person, or to Jesus? If you read the book of Isaiah, the Servant appears to be Israel or a prophet who represents Israel, but the prophecy took on a whole life of its own among Jews and Christians of the succeeding centuries. Christians quite naturally identify Isaiah 53 as talking about Jesus! Therefore, texts can and do mean a great deal more than an author might have intended. Texts can carry meaning in addition to what an author originally intended, and a text can also activate a certain meaning for readers far beyond what an author may have imagined when that text touches on a particular set of experiences. There is nothing radical or strange about this point. It merely confirms what we all know: meaning is a matter of context. Reading some of the biblical commands about slavery (e.g., Leviticus 19:20; 25:44–46; Deuteronomy 23:15) will evoke different things for white Anglo-Saxon settlers in nineteenth-century colonial America than for twenty-first-century, multicultural, urban American churches.

Inside the Text?

For other people, meaning is about the story, rhetoric, and dynamics **inside a text**. Meaning is entirely independent of the author's intention and is found exclusively in the text with its various possibilities. The task of interpretation, then, is to discover the storied features and persuasive power of a text. Forget the author, just let the text speak for itself! However, it seems strange to read a text without respect for the intention of an author and without an examination of how readers respond to it. I'm sure a first-time reading of *Romeo and Juliet* would be a very interesting experience for someone who has never heard of Shakespeare. They could plot the emotion, romance, and tragedy of the story.

And yet, whether we like it or not, it is hard to imagine making sense of Shakespearean plays without respect to Shakespeare himself, Elizabethan England and its literature, and the domain of Shakespeare studies. Texts are not toddlers; they cannot wander around as they like, do as they like, rant and rave as they like; no, texts have a parent in their author and guardians in their readers.

Hands of the Readers?

Then, for other people, meaning has nothing to do with the author or even the text; it is **all about the reader**. Authors are inaccessible, texts have no predetermined meaning, so meaning is created by the act of reading. For a cheeky example, scholar Dale Martin likes to illustrate this point by putting a Bible on a speaker's podium, stepping back, and inviting people to listen to what the Bible "says" to them. After a few moments of embarrassing silence, he likes to say, "Apparently, the Bible can't talk," by which he means, "Texts don't 'say' anything: they must be read."[1] Martin believes that although authors have intentions, nevertheless the authorial intention is not identical with the meaning of the text. Meaning is not constrained by the author or the text, but by the social context and community of the reader, who is drawn toward certain ways of reading and pushed toward particular interpretations.[2] For advocates of reader-centred approaches to interpreting Scripture, you can have multiple readings but no single "right" reading of a text

---

1. Dale Martin, *Sex and the Single Savior: Gender and Sexuality in Biblical Interpretation* (Louisville, KY: Westminster John Knox, 2006), 5.

2. Martin, *Sex and the Single Savior*, 6, 14–15.

because every person and community has their own truth which they can find in the text. This results in an explosion of diverse approaches to reading the Bible where the Bible means something different for every person or every group. You can have feminist, queer, African American, postcolonial, womanist, liberationist, and Marxist interpretation. The possibilities are limitless; you could even have an evangelical-Estonian-ecological-emo reading of Leviticus that is just as valid as anybody else's reading of Leviticus. Or else, you could retreat to a type of strict individualism: "This is what the Bible means to me, what it says to my heart, and how it speaks to me."

Now, we should admit that texts can be, in a sense, open—carrying all sorts of possibilities of meaning, eliciting a range of responses from diverse readers, and being read differently within varying communities. There is no question that your personal situation, your location, your culture, your history, and any groups you belong to shape the way you read books like the Bible. I take that as self-evident, and a good thing, as reading the Bible through the eyes of others can be extraordinarily enriching.

The problem is that a strict reader-centred approach to finding meaning in a text presupposes that readers are autonomous and absolute, while texts are nothing more than a mirror or echo chamber. If so, then all you see or hear in a text is what you and your community bring with you. Yet it seems obvious that reading is a transforming experience precisely because there is something "other" in the text, something other than ourselves, which challenges us and changes us in our act of reading. It becomes possible to read against the presuppositions of one's own community and to use texts to critique one's own context, to contest certain norms, and even to challenge one's own way of thinking! Besides, how do we correct bad or wrong readers if not by reference to the author and the text? How do you reject, say, a reading of the Bible that supports slavery, segregation, violence, and oppression, if not by reference to the author, text, and other readers? If the reader is always right because that is "true for them," then you can't critique or challenge any interpretation because all interpretations are treated as equally valid and as self-validating. We are forced into the position that biblical injunctions against the Hebrews marrying Canaanites (e.g., Deuteronomy 7:2–4; Joshua 23:12–13; Ezra 9:14) can be used to legitimize prejudice toward interracial couples if that is the framework or presupposition that some readers have! Yet the Bible compels us to act in certain ways, often against our culture, against our assumptions, against our own communities—seen particularly in the commands to love God and love our neighbour—so a text can and does place limits on the meanings that readers can take away from it.

Where Is Meaning?

So where does meaning reside: author, text, or reader? In my mind, interpretation—accessing what we call **"meaning"** **—is about the fusion of all three horizons together**. We take into account the *intention* of authors, the *dynamics* within texts, and the *understanding* of readers, and what we call "meaning" occurs in the fusion of all three. Ultimately, meaning is the web of connections we make with the world behind the text (the author's horizon), the world inside the text (the literary horizon), and the world we inhabit in front of the text (the reader's horizon). The more connections we make and the thicker those connections appear to be, the more preferable a particular meaning ascribed to the text becomes because it explains more of the features that surround our reading experience.[3]

Accordingly, a good interpretation, or a preferential form of meaning, is something that makes sense of an author's intention in his or her historical context, whether ancient Israel or the early church; it is something that explains and accounts for all the assertions and descriptions inside a text; and it is something that is eminently relatable to us readers. In the big picture, meaning includes what the author would say to us now, how the biblical texts challenge and energize us, and how our churches today imagine responding to a given text.

TIPS FOR INTERPRETATION

One of the tips I give to laypeople and students for understanding a biblical text is the catchphrase "C4." No, I don't mean a type of plastic explosives. Rather, I mean four words beginning with the letter *c*: context, content, concern, and contemporary application. C4 is what you should be mindful of as you read the Bible.

---

3. See Anthony C. Thiselton, *The Two Horizons: New Testament Hermeneutics and Philosophical Description with Special Reference to Heidegger, Bultmann, Gadamer and Wittgenstein* (Grand Rapids: Eerdmans, 1980), 439–40.

Context

First, there is the importance of **context**. Well-known Methodist scholar Ben Witherington loves to say, "A text without a context is just a pretext for whatever you want it to mean."[4] Such a line is worth memorizing because we all know the problem of taking something out of context, be it a line from a book, a joke, something from a former historical period, or pretty much any comment I make about my wife's cooking. Context is really the king of interpretation because context is the historical and literary atmosphere in which communication takes place. All communication is contextual and is shaped by multiple contexts including the historical setting of a text, a text's own literary environments, and the wider canonical context.

Ben Witherington demonstrates how attention to context can help one avoid strange interpretations:

I had a phone call over twenty years ago from a parishioner from one of my four N.C. Methodist Churches in the middle of the state. He wanted to know if it was o.k. to breed dogs, 'cause his fellow carpenter had told him that it said somewhere in the KJV that God's people shouldn't do that. I told him I would look up all the references to dog in the Bible and get to the bottom of this. There was nothing of any relevance in the NT, but then I came across this peculiar translation of an OT verse—"Thou shalt not breed with the dogs."

---

4. Ben Witherington, *The Living Word of God: Rethinking the Theology of the Bible* (Waco, TX: Baylor University Press, 2009), 70.

I called my church member up and told him, "I've got good news and bad news for you." He asked for the good news first. I said, "Well, you can breed as many of those furry four-footed creatures as you like, nothing in the Bible against it." He then asked what the bad news was. "Well," I said, "there is this verse that calls foreign women 'dogs' and warns the Israelites not to breed with them." There was a pregnant silence on the other end of the line, and finally Mr. Smith said, "Well, I am feeling much relieved; my wife Betty Sue is from just down the road in Chatham County!"[5]

We have already noted the importance of knowing some **historical context** in chapter 4 about the back-then-ness of biblical texts. If we are wise Bible readers, then we know that we are dealing with ancient documents and the proper way to grasp them, to get inside them, and to make the most of them is to understand these texts in the context of antiquity. That means, among other things, availing yourself of resources to help you understand a text in its own historical setting.

We must also understand a text's **literary context,** that is, its immediate literary setting. This is paramount for garnering a proper interpretation of a text. Otherwise, you end up just randomly ripping words out of context and using

---

5. Ben Witherington, "Hermeneutics—What Is It, and Why Do Bible Readers Need It?," *Ben Witherington on the Bible and Culture*, www.beliefnet.com/columnists/bibleandculture/2008/10/hermeneuticswhat-is-it-and-why-do-bible-readers-need-it.html.

them in whatever crazy manner you wish. I giggle to myself whenever I see a church that has a sign out front with the memorable words of Psalm 46:10, "Be still, and know that I am God." Many pastors and church folks treat this verse as if it says one should chill out for a moment away from the busyness of life, stop and relax, find a quiet spot, enjoy some serenity and peace, and reflect on how wonderful God is. The problem is that inner peace and feelings of tranquility have nothing to do with that verse. It is all about sitting back and watching God smash your enemies because he will not allow the nations who oppose Jacob's children to triumph over them. Yes, be still and know that God is God . . . as he unleashes apocalyptic judgment on your adversaries. Or consider Matthew 18:20 where Jesus said, "For where two or three gather in my name, there am I with them." So even if only two or three people attend the prayer meeting or the vicar's luncheon, God is still with you. Maybe, but in Matthew 18 the discourse is about church discipline and excommunication. When two or three gather together to dish out some discipline to a wayward member of the church, yes, God is indeed with them. One final example is Jesus's well-known invitation in Revelation 3:20: "Here I am! I stand at the door and knock. If anyone hears my voice and opens the door, I will come in and eat with that person, and they with me." These poignant words have been used in many evangelistic tracts and evangelistic sermons; however, they are actually part of a call for deeper fellowship with Christ issued to the church in Laodicea, not an evangelistic invitation.

There is also **canonical context**, meaning that we read

each book of the Bible not as a standalone document but as part of a larger and distinct literary body, the biblical canon. Every biblical text has its place within the single storyline of redemptive history as laid out from Genesis to Revelation. This has implications for how we regard passages like Genesis 3:15 (Eve's offspring will crush the serpent's head) and its projected fulfilment in Jesus according to Revelation 12 (Christ and the people of God will defeat the dragon). Also, the pessimism about life after death in Ecclesiastes 9 needs to be counterbalanced with the hope for eternal life in the Gospel of John, Romans 8:31–39, and Revelation 21–22. Our interpretation of one part of Scripture needs to be informed, balanced, or even corrected by our reading of other parts.

Of course, by taking this canonical approach there is a danger here that we flatten what is distinctive in a biblical book or impose upon it the conclusions of our wider canonical readings! Let me tell you, I've had students insist that Daniel 7, with its description of the coming of the Son of Man, just absolutely, truly, most definitely has to be about Jesus's second coming because Matthew 24 is the proper interpretation of Daniel 7. To be honest, I think Daniel 7 has nothing to do with Jesus's second coming; it is about the vindication of God's people, God's kingdom, and God's messianic king over and against the pagan world. I've also heard sermons preached on the Gospel of Matthew and the ideas and themes expounded by the preacher sound peculiarly Pauline rather than Matthean, as if Matthew were just a pseudonym for Paul. Sadly, a lot of canonical interpretation does not really end up connecting Daniel with

Matthew or connecting Matthew with Paul; it ends up just distorting the first biblical text by awkwardly reading another biblical text into it. It is a trap we all fall into at one time or another.

We can also point out that certain canonical tensions call for resolution. For example, there are God's commandments to kill Israel's tribal enemies in Deuteronomy versus Jesus's teaching to love our enemies in Matthew. Paul makes impassioned arguments for justification by faith whereas James contends that faith alone does not justify. Or calls to preserve Israel's ethnic purity in Ezra grate against Paul's claim that the church should be a fellowship of multiethnic believers. We should be unsurprised by these textual tensions because the Bible is not so much a single book as it is a library of Israel's national and religious history, the story of Jesus, and the literary residue of the beginnings of the Christian church. So we can expect some diversity to be normal with such a multiplicity of voices found in the Bible.

But here's the chief principle for us to consider: let each text be itself, try to understand it on its own terms, take its individuality seriously, but after that, don't be afraid to put it in conversation with the wider biblical canon. It is in fact desirable that we use the whole of the biblical canon to mutually interpret the individual parts. If we got Isaiah, Haggai, Paul, Luke, and John together to have a conversation on the meaning of creation, salvation, ethics, worship, or love, what would each one bring to the conversation? That is canonical interpretation! Using canonical context means that we pursue just how each biblical text is genuinely illuminated, fulfilled, or perfected by reading it beside all the other biblical texts. Taking a canonical approach means letting each part of the scriptural canon speak for itself, but also using Scripture to interpret Scripture, weaving together any apparent textual conflicts to bring about a canonical consensus. This canonical approach is the true essence of Protestant interpretation! The early Reformers were concerned with reading Scripture in light of the overarching storyline of Scripture. They were concerned with letting Scripture interpret Scripture rather than allowing it to be settled by a long chain of tradition that climaxed in the latest declarations of the Holy See. Scripture is what gave the Reformers leverage against the perceived corruption of the medieval church and its misrepresentation of Jesus and the apostles.

So context—historical, literary, and canonical—is vitally important for interpretation; thus you should always read a text with these three contexts in mind.

Content

Second, there is **content**, where you engage in a close reading of the biblical text, analyse the main subjects that a text is referring to, and identify the many literary devices that the text contains. There are many components to content, and I shall explore some of them below.

Genre is worth knowing about. Genre can refer to things like a style, type, theme, perspective, or category of something in art, music, and literature. We could say that genre is a set of recognizable textual features that carries clues to the author's intention while also activating expectations in the reader of how a text is supposed to be understood. Genre is like a prearranged contract between author and reader about how the rules of meaning will be applied in the reading of the text. Genre tells us how a text relates to the author and to reality and how it is to be applied. A book that begins, "Once upon a time . . . ," should be interpreted differently than a label on a plastic container that says, "Take three times a day with meals." In reading biblical texts, knowing the genre of a historical narrative, a psalm, a proverb, a prophetic book, a Gospel, a letter, or an apocalypse will help us understand how the text relates to reality and how we are to relate to it. Wrestling with a biblical text means knowing the importance of genre and understanding how the genre of the biblical text you are reading functions with its many conventions. In fact, I would say that knowing something about the genre of ancient Near Eastern creation stories is vital for understanding Genesis 1–3 and knowing about Jewish apocalyptic writings is mandatory for getting your head around the book of Revelation. Otherwise you run the risk of making category mistakes and taking something literally when it is meant to be understood figuratively, or taking something figuratively when it should be understood literally. Knowing the genre of a biblical book, and knowing the conventions and expectations of a given genre, helps avoid many mistakes of interpretation.

Tracking a **story** is important for any analysis of the Bible because many parts of the Bible from Genesis to Revelation are a story. This can include characterization, plot, tension, the point of view of the narrator, editorial asides, irony, humour, repetition of themes, tragedy, and so forth.

The aim is to understand how the story moves along—where the tensions reside, where the resolution is—and to imagine the impact that the story is intended to have upon readers. As we read biblical stories, whether from 1 Kings or Jesus's parables, the challenge for readers is to understand how the story creates meaning and how we should appropriate the story for ourselves today.

Rhetorical features need to be observed because the Bible contains its own set of rhetorical characteristics. By rhetoric I don't mean hot air or exaggeration; rather, I mean how parts of the Bible seek to persuade, not merely to impart information to someone, but to move them toward a certain point of view. For example, in the major prophets and in the New Testament epistles, you find units that use a mixture of poetic prose and emotive language to persuade readers to think in a certain way, to undertake particular actions, or to adopt a certain perspective. In Romans 8, Paul's aim through his intricately woven argument was to fill readers with hope, to drive them to resist the flesh and to follow the lead of the Spirit, to understand their own place in the divine story of salvation, and to inspire them with a vision of God's love. Or think about the book of Jeremiah, where the prophet confronted readers through dramatic prose filled with similes and metaphors about God's covenant-love for the exiles and explained how God intends to end their time of mourning, to restore the nation, and to inaugurate a new covenant. Readers need to pay attention to how the Bible, through imagery and argument, commands and metaphor, tries to persuade them to adopt a certain point of view or a particular form of behavior.

DID YOU KNOW?

The five Old Testament passages most cited and alluded to in the New Testament are the following:

1. Psalm 110:1
2. Leviticus 19:18
3. Psalm 2:6
4. Psalm 118:22–23
5. Daniel 7:13–14

Attentive readers should pay attention to **intertextuality,** which is how a biblical book refers to other biblical books. Every text is, in some way, a dialogue with a previous text. We experience this in our own culture. If we suspect that someone is lying, we might hint that their nose is growing longer, alluding to the story of Pinocchio. Similarly, biblical texts can evoke prior biblical texts. For example, Jeremiah's prophecy that the exiles will languish in Babylon for "seventy years" (Jeremiah 25:11–12; 29:10) is evoked by Daniel in "seventy 'sevens,'" or 490 years, to deal with sin and to establish atonement (Daniel 9:24). Or when Paul says that "Christ, our Passover Lamb, has been sacrificed," he evokes the story of the exodus and the first Passover (Exodus 12; 1 Corinthians 5:7). Likewise, Jesus's response to Caiaphas at his trial, "You will see the Son of Man sitting at the right hand of the Mighty One and coming on the clouds of heaven" (Mark 14:62), alludes to Daniel 7:13, about one like a Son of Man coming to the Ancient of Days, and to

Psalm 110:1, about a Davidic king being enthroned beside Israel's Lord. Sometimes intertextuality can be very dramatic and very important, such as when Jesus says, "Before Abraham was born, 'I am'" (John 8:58), which is a throwback to the Lord announcing his name to Moses as "I am who I am" (Exodus 3:14). So it is vital that, when reading the Bible, one is constantly looking at where and how biblical texts are quoted, biblical stories are alluded to, and biblical themes are echoed and reworked. These intertextual passages are great cues for what biblical authors are trying to do (see the appendix at the end of the book, "The Top Five Old Testament Texts in the New Testament").

A significant feature of the content of any biblical text is the various **exhortations** and **commands** that are made by authors. Biblical writers tell people to engage in certain behaviors and to abstain from others, to think and act a certain way, or to put a certain attitude or action far from their mind. One of the easiest things to do in a Bible study on an instructional text like Proverbs or 1 John is to underline all the words that issue commands and set out expectations. Then try to determine whether the commands are directly transferable to us, are transferable by analogy, require cultural reinterpretation, or are limited to the original context.

For example, "You shall not murder" (Exodus 20:13) is directly transferable; never good to murder people, always bad. "I, Paul, tell you that if you let yourselves be circumcised, Christ will be of no value to you at all" (Galatians 5:2) is transferable by analogy; while you're unlikely to meet Jewish proselytizers in your congregation ordering the men to get circumcised to ensure their full conversion, certain persons on the margins of your church might try to advocate some weird mix of moralism and legalism as a way to win God's favour. "Every man who prays or prophesies with his head covered dishonors his head" (1 Corinthians 11:4), definitely requires cultural reinterpretation; no one is going to confuse you as a worshipper of Greek and Roman gods if you pray with a hat, hoodie, or toupee. This exhortation can be transferred to a general principle: don't adopt a mode of piety that looks like it's a variation of modern pagan practices, and make sure the substance and style of your worship honors God. A good reader of Scripture will pay due attention to its many commands and discern how those commands are applicable and relevant to us and the church today.

In sum, when it comes to content, we need to know about biblical genres, what they are, how they work, and what we should pay particular attention to. Knowing about genre can help us avoid making a lot of mistakes. It is necessary, too, to pay attention to biblical stories: how they develop plot, character, and tension and how they come to a resolution. Focus especially on how God appears and functions in the story. In more instructional texts, learn how to trace arguments, noting the main points, the reasoning and rhetorical features, and what makes the argument persuasive. A big thing is intertextuality, or how biblical texts quote and allude to other biblical texts. This is especially important because so much of the NT is based on a rehearsal of OT themes. Finally, pay attention to commands and exhortations. Then, with your church, friends, and family, discern whether and how such commands can be lived out in your own context.

Concern

I know it might sound very basic, but it always helps interpreters, when they try to move beyond the many details in order to find the big idea behind the text, to discover what is the **main concern**. To put it simply, ask these questions: What is the author getting at through the text? Why has the author written this text this way? And what type of response was the author trying to activate in the reader? This is similar to finding the purpose. But beyond that, what type of impact did the author envisage his or her text having on the readers and toward what end?

Another simple tip is to ask, "If we did not have this particular verse, paragraph, or passage, what would we be missing?" It is useful to be able to read a biblical text and identify the main idea as well as the author's aim and motivation in writing. I don't mean second-guessing motives or exposing a secret agenda lurking underneath the text; rather, I mean no more than asking what type of God-shaped way of life the author is trying to persuade readers about through this biblical text.

For example, I would say that Matthew's primary concern in the Sermon on the Mount (Matthew 5–7) is to set out Jesus's teaching in a way that accents a fulfilment of OT themes but also emphasizes the newness of his teaching. Jesus is not just giving the Law of Moses 2.0; this is the manifesto for the kingdom of heaven. This is a new law for a renewed Israel, for a people of the new age. Or to give another example, the main concern of Mark 15 is not only to narrate the story of Jesus's crucifixion but to show through the repetition of regal language—repeating the words "king" and "messiah"—that this is how the kingdom comes in power, this is Jesus the Servant King, this is the Son of Man who gives his life as a ransom for many. Readers need to develop the habit of moving beyond what is being said to looking for what the author is getting at!

Contemporary Application

Last but by no means least we can focus on **contemporary application**. Application is the point where we ask, "So what?" or "How does this text change anything I believe or do?" In many biblical texts, it is about receiving a basic working knowledge of God and God's actions: God is good and gracious, God brought the Hebrews out of Egypt, God was unhappy with King Saul, Jesus commanded Paul to preach his name to the gentiles, etc. In other instances, it is a matter of do this and don't do that: help the poor and don't commit adultery. And yet, beyond the rudimentary *know this* and *do/don't do that*, we can imagine many more ways of applying the Bible to our lives.

WORST APPLICATION EVER!

In my time, I've heard of some of the crazy ways that people try to apply the Bible. Sometimes weird, sometimes wrong, sometimes cringeworthy. One particularly *odd* application that I was told about, admittedly secondhand, concerns a pastor who allegedly preached on Joshua 6 about the fall of the walls of Jericho, and his application was to this effect: "Men, if you are single, if there is a woman here whom you feel God is leading you toward marrying, then I invite you to walk around her seven times and blow your trumpet, and the walls of her heart will crumble before you." There is allegory and then there is crazy stuff like that. My advice, if you ever find someone walking around you seven times, unless you're at an athletics track, run far and run fast!

First, we can explore how a biblical text leads us to a bigger view of God and God's purposes, especially in relation to the church and the world. Biblical texts like Ephesians 1, with Paul's thanksgivings and prayer, demonstrate how rich and full of wisdom God's plan is. Similarly, Revelation 5, with the vision of Jesus as the Lamb of God *and* Lion of Judah, is a powerful and vivid portrayal of Jesus as the one who executes God's plan, hidden before the ages, to unite himself with creation through the eternal Son. Texts like these really do enlarge our view of God, proving that God is not a distant deity but is the glorious Father, who is Alpha and Omega, the one in whom we live and move and have our being, the God who will be all in all. Application is partly marveling at the majesty of God as he is presented to us in Scripture.

Second, we can pursue how a biblical text shapes our walk with Christ and our life in the way of Christ. Biblical texts can, in manifold ways, speak to us directly, comfort us in times of sorrow or anxiety, rebuke us for wrongful behavior, call us to deeper intimacy with God, and make us conscious of the Spirit's leadings. Scripture also puts us in a place to live faithfully and to live differently from the world. It urges us to make sure our talk matches our walk. Scripture guides us in how to live genuinely and authentically as Christians.

Third, contemporary application also requires a scripturally shaped imagination. One exercise I do when teaching courses on the Gospels is to urge students to tell their own version of Luke 15:11–32. I tell them to give a contemporary expression of the parable of the prodigal son, where they have to give their own short story about a loving father, a wayward son or daughter, and a resentful older sibling, all in order to underscore the nature of God's scandalous grace to those who don't deserve it. Ultimately, the best applications are those that provide a wise mixture of faithfulness to the biblical world and creative imagination as to how a biblical text becomes freshly relevant for us today.

BEING A BETTER BIBLE READER

I hope this chapter has given you some useful insights into the complexity of interpreting biblical texts. We've seen how the meaning of a biblical text is really the careful integration of an author's intention, the textual content itself, and the many responses made by readers to a biblical text. I've offered you my own set of tips for how to practically unpack a biblical text using C4: *context* (exploring a text's historical, literary, and canonical setting), *content* (investigating a text's genre, story, argument, intertextuality, and commands), *concern* (identifying an author's primary agenda), and *contemporary application* (asking, "So what?" after a careful reading of the text).

RECOMMENDED READING

Fee, Gordon D., and Douglas K. Stuart. *How to Read the Bible for All Its Worth*. Grand Rapids: Zondervan, 2014.

Harvey, Angela Lou. *Spiritual Reading: A Study of the Christian Practice of Reading Scripture*. United Kingdom: James Clarke, 2016.

Strauss, Mark. *How to Read the Bible in Changing Times: Understanding and Applying God's Word Today*. Grand Rapids: Baker, 2011.

Wright, N. T. *Scripture and the Authority of God: How to Read the Bible Today*. New York: HarperOne, 2011.

6

THE PURPOSE OF SCRIPTURE IS KNOWLEDGE, FAITH, LOVE, AND HOPE

I love a good "life hack." You know, those cute bits of advice that give you shortcuts to become more productive and efficient and that take some of the hassle out of life. The other day I found a great life hack that showed me how to use my phone to take a picture of a page in a book and then convert the picture into a Word doc so I don't have to type out all the words. Brilliant! It saved me many minutes of typing. There are also great life hacks for parents. My personal favourite—if toddlers won't stay in their room at night, put a sock on their doorknob with a rubber band to keep it on. That way the kid cannot grip the doorknob tight enough to open the door. I've done this, it works, though you inevitably end up with toddlers going to sleep crying at the entrance to their room. But yeah, I love a good life hack.

Be that as it may, Scripture is not a divine list of life hacks. Yes, it contains some great tips on everything from parenting to work habits to marriage and much more. The book of Proverbs and the letter of James both contain practical advice for *how* to live wisely and faithfully before God and others. But Scripture was not written to help you lose weight, find a better career, be more productive in the office, be a better you, or even discover yourself. Yes, the Christian Scriptures can help us with the mundane elements of life, but Scripture's true purpose transcends the mundane and draws us into the mystery of God's person, God's love, and God's promises to put all things under Christ's reign. The purpose and power of Scripture are experienced in the discipline of immersing oneself daily into the mystery of God as he reveals himself in his word.

It is Scripture, under the Holy Spirit's guidance, and with the tutelage of our church's traditions, that enables us to achieve genuine and lasting transformation. It is by soaking ourselves in Scripture that we cultivate virtue, curate our character, and conform ourselves to the pattern of Christ. You can describe this in technical theological words like "sanctification" (i.e., becoming holier) or with general descriptions like "godliness" (i.e., becoming more like God in our character). If we engage in consistent and wise readings of the Bible, individually and communally, then hopefully we will reap many of the benefits of marinating our minds in Scripture.

To put it briefly, I like to say that the purpose of Scripture is that God's people would attain the knowledge of God, deepen their faith, abound in love for God and love for others, and enjoy the assurance of hope—these are things we get from Scripture!

KNOWING GOD

One purpose of Scripture is to know God: to know who God is, what God does, God's purpose for creation, his purpose to put all things under Christ and for the church to reign with Christ over the new creation. This means, as you might expect, that there is much to know about God! Fortunately for us, God is the God who makes himself known. It is in the Bible that God's revelation of himself is put into written form; that is, God inspired authors to communicate his divine will through a written medium. The Scriptures, in their diverse ways, contain God's message to us, wisdom for a way of life under God. **Knowledge of God begins with knowledge of Scripture; so the more you know of Scripture, the more you know of God.** This knowledge is necessary if we are to have a relationship with God, to be in covenant with him, to be his children, to know his Son, Jesus Christ, and to experience the illuminating work of the Holy Spirit. A lack of knowledge is not just ignorance; it is alienation from God, estrangement from God's love, and separation from God's offer of reconciliation. As Hosea said in his own time, "My people perish for want of knowledge" (Hosea 4:6 NJB).

Across the breadth of Scripture, we see numerous examples where knowing God comes by knowing Scripture. This knowledge is the knowledge of God's covenant-love, God's commands, and God's plan for his people. The Lord instructed Joshua to tell the Israelites to "keep this Book of the Law always on your lips; meditate on it day and night, so that you may be careful to do everything written in it. Then you will be prosperous and successful" (Joshua 1:8). The basis for this command is straightforward: keeping faith with God meant keeping the commandments, which required knowing Scripture, and knowing Scripture meant teaching Scripture to the people. Obviously, if we thirst for knowledge of God, then we must thirst for his word, thirst for the knowledge that comes from Scripture. Along this line, the psalmist urges us to impress God's word into the very fabric of our lives: "How can a young person stay on the path of purity? By living according to your word. I seek you with all my heart; do not let me stray from your commands. I have hidden your word in my heart that I might not sin against you" (Psalm 119:9–11). When Israel fell into disobedience, it was the rediscovery of the Law under Josiah and then again under Ezra which brought repentance, reformation, and renewal to the Jewish people (see 2 Kings 23; Ezra 7; Nehemiah 8). God's word in the Law continually reminded the Israelites of God's covenant-love for them, God's purposes for them, and God's commands to them. The rediscovery of the Law brought the nation out of the morass of judgment and exile and back into God's blessings and favour.

What is a Christian? J. I. Packer writes:

What is a Christian? Christians can be described from many angles, but from what we have said we can cover everything by saying: True Christians are people who acknowledge and live under the word of God. They submit without reserve to the word of God written in the "Book of Truth" (Dan. 10:21), believing the teaching, trusting the promises, following the commands. Their eyes are on the God of the Bible as their Father, and the Christ of the Bible as their Saviour. They will tell you, if you ask them, that the word of God has both convinced them of sin and assured them of forgiveness. Their consciences, like Luther's, are captive to the word of God, and they aspire, like the psalmist, to have their whole life brought into line with it. "Oh, that my ways were steadfast in obeying your decrees!" "Do not let me stray from your commands." "Teach me your decrees. Let me understand the teaching of your precepts." "May my heart be blameless toward your decrees" (Ps. 119:5, 10, 26f., 36, 80). The promises are before them as they pray, and the precepts are before them as they go about their daily tasks.[1]

In Paul's opening to his letter to the Ephesians, he prays a specific prayer for them: "I keep asking that the God of our Lord Jesus Christ, the glorious Father, may give you the Spirit of wisdom and revelation, so that you may know

---

1. J. I. Packer, *Knowing God* (London: Hodder & Stoughton, 2013), 130.

him better" (Ephesians 1:17).[2] That is the purpose of reading Scripture, studying it, meditating on it, and preaching from it: to know God better. What we know better is, among other things, that "God is God; he is the faithful God, keeping his covenant of love" (Deuteronomy 7:9); "It is he who made us, and we are his, we are his people, the sheep of his pasture (Psalm 100:3); and "God is love, and those who abide in love abide in God, and God abides in them" (1 John 4:16 NRSV). Through our reading of Scripture, and the knowledge of God that it gives us, we begin to grasp ever more profoundly the love and beauty of the God who knows us and loves us.

Therefore, the goal of our instruction in the Scriptures is to know God better so that we may grow in our love for God. As theologian Ellen T. Charry comments, "By knowing God, we come to love him, and by loving him we come to know him."[3] This emphasis on knowing does not mean trying to replace faith with facts; rather, it means something like seeking a deeper knowledge of God through a faith informed by learning—not a purely rational knowing, but growth into a closer relationship with God. It is a knowledge that abounds in love, thanksgiving, and praise.

Knowing God through Scripture is important because, as the French Reformer John Calvin understood, without knowledge of God, there is no knowledge of self.[4] It is by

---

2. See D. A. Carson, *Praying with Paul: A Call to Spiritual Reformation*, 2nd ed. (Grand Rapids: Baker, 2004), 150–55.

3. Ellen T. Charry, *By the Renewing of Your Minds: The Pastoral Function of Christian Doctrine* (New York: Oxford University Press, 1999), 4.

4. Calvin, *Institutes of the Christian Religion*, I.1.1.

knowing God, or more importantly, by being known *by* God, that we can know who we are—in relationship to God, in relationship to the church, and in relationship to the world (see 1 Corinthians 8:3; 13:12; Galatians 4:9).[5] **So the first purpose of Scripture is knowledge of God.** More than mere agreement with certain facts, it is more properly a relational knowledge, a knowledge to save us, to make us wise, and to form us according to the image of Jesus and the eternal word of God.

FAITH

One thing that Scripture does—no surprises here—is **bring people to a point of faith.** According to St. John the Evangelist, the purpose of his Gospel is evangelical: "These [things] are written that you may believe that Jesus is the Messiah, the Son of God, and that by believing you may have life in his name" (John 20:31). The notion that the evangelists like John wrote books that are "evangelical," in that they set forth the gospel-story of Jesus and call for a faith-response to him, is kind of a no-brainer. In fact, when I first encountered Christianity and the Bible, one verse from John's Gospel that I found particularly startling and confronting—and which elicited the first murmurs of faith—was Jesus's words in his speech directed at the Judean leaders: "Very truly I tell you, whoever hears my word and believes him who sent me has eternal life and will not be

---

5. See the important work in this regard by Brian S. Rosner, *Known by God: A Biblical Theology of Personal Identity* (Grand Rapids: Zondervan, 2017).

judged but has crossed over from death to life" (John 5:24). I saw here the promise of eternal life, the benefits of faith, and I experienced that kind of magnetic attraction to Jesus that the Gospels furnish by so wonderfully conveying the story and words of Jesus. My story is not unique. I have heard countless testimonies of people who came to faith, seemingly from nowhere, by picking up a Bible. Whether a Gideons Bible in a hotel room, a friend's Bible in a college dorm, or a few verses quoted in an email from a friend. This is precisely what God's word does—it creates faith from the darkness of disbelief and despair, and it plants the seeds that grow into trust in God, love for Christ, and listening to the Spirit. Or as the apostle Paul said: "Faith comes from hearing the message, and the message is heard through the word about Christ" (Romans 10:17). Scripture is without a doubt the most successful evangelist there is, was, or will be!

The other thing Scripture does is **bring us to a deepening faith**. Scripture provides us with instruction in how to live a life that glorifies God, avoids sin, prepares for the kingdom, and imitates Christ. But, as I've said, Scripture is not just a user's manual or a book of "how to" tips on the religious life. Scripture brings us to a deeper knowledge of God's character and closer intimacy with God's person. Through Scripture we can pray with more assurance to "Abba" our Father, to Christ our Brother, and to the Holy Spirit our Comforter. Scripture makes God more real to us. Scripture constantly assures us that God is for us. Scripture reiterates the hope that is ours in Christ Jesus. The best example of someone basking in Scripture that I can think of is at the end of Psalm 119. This psalm is the longest chapter in Scripture, and it celebrates the comfort that only God's word can provide. This is how the psalm ends:

> I rejoice in your promise
>   like one who finds great spoil.
> I hate and detest falsehood
>   but I love your law.
> Seven times a day I praise you
>   for your righteous laws.
> Great peace have those who love your law,
>   and nothing can make them stumble.
> I wait for your salvation, Lord,
>   and I follow your commands.
> I obey your statutes,
>   for I love them greatly.
> I obey your precepts and your statutes,
>   for all my ways are known to you.
>
> May my cry come before you, Lord;
>   give me understanding according to your word.
> May my supplication come before you;
>   deliver me according to your promise.
> May my lips overflow with praise,
>   for you teach me your decrees.
> May my tongue sing of your word,
>   for all your commands are righteous.
> May your hand be ready to help me,
>   for I have chosen your precepts.
> I long for your salvation, Lord,
>   and your law gives me delight.

> Let me live that I may praise you,
>> and may your laws sustain me.
> I have strayed like a lost sheep.
>> Seek your servant,
>> for I have not forgotten your commands.
>>> (Psalm 119:162–176)

While the psalmist is talking about the Law here (i.e., the first five books of the Old Testament), the sense of delight applies to the entire biblical canon. Scripture teaches us God's ways. It elicits our praise, makes us rejoice, and assures us of God's deliverance. Scripture draws us closer to God, and the closer to God we get, the more we delight in his holy word. I really dislike those cheesy descriptions of Scripture as a "love letter from God," but Scripture is a mode of God's presence with us. It is God's living word, a word alive with his voice, infused with his love, and illuminated by his promises that speaks to us throughout our lives. It is a word that calls, comforts, and counsels like a Father speaking to his children or like a mother tending to her young. It is in this holy word that we know who God is and who we are in relationship with God.

I think it is important to stress that knowledge about God is not enough; it is knowledge of God in tandem with faith in God that matters. Going back to the Gospel of John, we need to take seriously Jesus's rebuke to the Jerusalem priests: "You study the Scriptures diligently because you think that in them you have eternal life. These are the very Scriptures that testify about me, yet you refuse to come to me to have life" (John 5:39–40). Anyone can learn about the

God of the Bible or about the theology of Christianity by studying Western religion, ancient Near Eastern civilizations, or comparative studies of Mediterranean deities. But, as Jesus points out, that is not the purpose of Scripture! The purpose of Scripture is not to help people get a passing grade in Religion 101. Rather, the purpose of Scripture is to bring people to believe in Jesus, to draw close to Jesus, to grasp hold of Jesus, to rest in the one whose yoke is easy and whose burden is light (Matthew 11:30). I'll have more on Jesus and Scripture in the next chapter. For now, you should note that **Scripture brings us to faith, to a wise faith, a holistic faith, and a deepening faith**.

> What does it mean for you to have faith? To have faith means that I believe the Gospel is the truth: that Jesus died for my sins, rose from the dead, and rules over my life. Therefore, I entrust myself to him as my Savior, and I obey him as my Lord.
>
> —*J. I. Packer and Joel Scandrett*, To Be a Christian: An Anglican Catechism *(Wheaton, IL: Crossway, 2020), 25.*

LOVE FOR GOD AND OTHERS

Another purpose of Scripture is love, which includes **growing in love for God and love for others**. Whereas many Christians imagine Israel's faith as dry, ritualistic, and legalistic, this is far from the case. Love was among the central facets of the faith of ancient Israel. Israel's most basic creed is the *shema*, which is really a call to love God with all of one's resources: "Love the LORD your God with all your heart and with all your soul and with all your strength" (Deuteronomy 6:5). Also in Deuteronomy, Moses instructed the Israelites: "For I command you today to love the LORD your God," which practically means that they are "to walk in obedience to him, and to keep his commands, decrees and laws," and if they do so, "then you will live and increase, and the LORD your God will bless you in the land you are entering to possess" (Deuteronomy 30:16). Love among the Israelites was designed to stop a culture of revenge and constant retribution, hence the words "love your neighbor as yourself" (Leviticus 19:18). What is more, this love command extends to foreigners and refugees: "The foreigner residing among you must be treated as your native-born. Love them as yourself, for you were foreigners in Egypt" (Leviticus 19:34). Among the purposes of the Law was to call the people to love God, to show them how to love God, and to charge them to love each other. Just as God has covenant-love for the Israelites, so too must the Israelites exercise covenant-love among themselves.

THE LOVE COMMAND IN THE NEW TESTAMENT

Jesus replied: "'Love the Lord your God with all your heart and with all your soul and with all your mind.' This is the first and greatest commandment. And the second is like it: 'Love your neighbor as yourself.' All the Law and the Prophets hang on these two commandments." (Matthew 22:37–40)

"My command is this: Love each other as I have loved you. Greater love has no one than this: to lay down one's life for one's friends." (John 15:12–13)

Let no debt remain outstanding, except the continuing debt to love one another, for whoever loves others has fulfilled the law. The commandments, "You shall not commit adultery," "You shall not murder," "You shall not steal," "You shall not covet," and whatever other command there may be, are summed up in this one command: "Love your neighbor as yourself." (Romans 13:8–9)

Above all, love each other deeply, because love covers over a multitude of sins. (1 Peter 4:8)

If you really keep the royal law found in Scripture, "Love your neighbor as yourself," you are doing right. (James 2:8)

Dear friends, since God so loved us, we also ought to love one another. No one has ever seen God; but if we love one another, God lives in us and his love is made complete in us. (1 John 4:11–12)

One of the distinctive features of Jesus's ministry was the role he assigned to love. The function of Scripture, when combined with Jesus's kingdom message, was to lead people into a double love: love for God and love for others. When a scribe asked Jesus, "Which is the greatest commandment?"

Jesus responded with an amalgamation of Deuteronomy 6:5 and Leviticus 19:18: "Jesus replied: 'Love the Lord your God with all your heart and with all your soul and with all your mind.' This is the first and greatest commandment. And the second is like it: 'Love your neighbor as yourself.' All the Law and the Prophets hang on these two commandments" (Matthew 22:36–40). For Jesus, this was the true meaning of Scripture, not a list of rules and regulations to manufacture a micropiety that covered every area of life. Scripture is meant to be experienced as a fountain gushing forth with God's love for us, our love for God, love for our brothers and sisters in Christ, and love for all people. This made Jesus stand out because, as New Testament scholar Scot McKnight observes, whereas the Pharisees taught a love for Torah, Jesus taught a Torah of love.[6]

I'm sure most of you know Paul's ode to love in 1 Corinthians 13, a famous text filled with some of the most memorable verses of Scripture:

> Love is patient, love is kind. It does not envy, it does not boast, it is not proud. It does not dishonor others, it is not self-seeking, it is not easily angered, it keeps no record of wrongs. Love does not delight in evil but rejoices with the truth. It always protects, always trusts, always hopes, always perseveres. Love never fails. But where there are prophecies, they will cease; where there are tongues, they will be stilled; where there is knowledge, it will pass away. (1 Corinthians 13:4–8)

6. Scot McKnight, *The Jesus Creed* (Brewster, MA: Paraclete, 2004), 53–54.

Now, most people seem to treat this passage as if Paul was writing to the Corinthians and then, all of a sudden, he dropped in a random sermon on the virtue of love so that one day Christians would have a sappy tearjerker text to read at weddings. Something that was spiritual enough to sound Christian, but not too preachy in a way that unchurched folks would find discomforting. But we should read this so-called wedding text in the context of 1 Corinthians 12–14.

When read in context, in 1 Corinthians 13:4–8, Paul is trying to adjudicate in a battle where people are arguing about the proper way to do worship—Whose worship is holier? Whose gifts are better? What is the hierarchy of gifts? and so forth. Amid all that ruckus—"Your spiritual gift is inferior to mine," "I'm more spiritual than you"—Paul's point is that the entire "war over worship" is simply missing the point. Paul reminds the Corinthians that worship needs to be led by the Spirit and not by egos, driven by the Spirit and not by popularity contests, and animated by the Spirit and not by the pursuit of status using spiritual currency. Moreover, what Paul really stresses is that if you want to talk about superspirituality, then the true measure of spirituality is the way of love and the greatest gift in the church is the gift of love in action. That is because love is the truest form of worship, love is the highest form of knowledge, and love is the supreme mode of spirituality. Whether it is prophecy or preaching, tongues or teaching, they need to embrace the most excellent way of love because love is the goal and measure of all things spiritual. Authentic worship and true spirituality are "love actually" (let fans of British romantic comedies understand!).

Scripture is jam-packed with teachings and themes about love: love for God, love for the church, and love for our neighbours. By reading Scripture, we discover the prominence of love in God's instruction to us, and we develop a Spirit-endowed desire to love God and to love others. It is through Scripture that we should feel compelled by our new nature, our spiritual nature, to heed Jesus's double love command to love God and to love others. Scripture encourages us to walk in the way of love because God in Christ first loved us.

I am personally allergic to trying to reduce Christianity to some kind of touchy-feely lovefest, where we all hold hands, share our feelings, and talk about hugging rainbows. But biblical interpretation is useless, futile, and even offensive to God when it is divorced from the virtue of love. For where there are Greek nouns and Hebrew verbs, they will be parsed and will pass. Where there are dictionaries of theology, they will soon be dated. Where there are theological tongues flapping about the minutiae of doctrine, they will be stilled. Where there are arguments over points of doctrine, they will be drowned out by the symphony of God's glory. In my experience, people are less likely to remember your exegesis, your sermon, or your Bible study than they are to remember your love for them or lack of love toward them. Your demonstration of love is the greatest sermon you will ever preach and the most lasting sermon anyone will ever remember. Or as John Wesley said, the Christian life is "the royal way of universal love."[7]

---

7. John Wesley, Sermon 39.

If the Bible were a seminary, love is the provost, and the curriculum has two main learning outcomes: love for God and love for your neighbour. Scripture talks so much about love because love is the test of true discipleship (John 13:34–35) and love is the true form of worship (1 Corinthians 13:4–8). Love matters for biblical interpretation because, as Augustine said, whoever "thinks that he understands the Holy Scriptures, or any part of them, but puts such an interpretation on them as does not tend to build up into this twofold love of God and neighbor, does not yet understand them as he ought."[8]

ENDURANCE UNTO HOPE

When I wrote my Romans commentary a few years back, one of the most striking things I learned and reflected upon was Paul's account of the purpose of Scripture. What do you think it is? Rules, religion, redemption, a relationship with God? Nope, not even close! Paul, while urging the "weak" and "strong" in the Roman assemblies to "welcome one another," added this pithy yet very profound comment about Scripture's purpose: "For everything that was written in the past was written to teach us, so that through the **endurance** taught in the Scriptures and the encouragement they provide we might have **hope**" (Romans 15:4). The purpose of Scripture according to Paul is to impart to us endurance and hope!

Endurance, according to Scripture, is "the capacity to

---

8. Augustine, *On Christian Doctrine* 1.36.

hold out or bear up in the face of difficulty," entailing the virtues of "patience, endurance, fortitude, steadfastness, perseverance."[9] Scripture is our coach, our nourishment, our inspiration, and our guide in a spiritual struggle as we steadily ebb closer toward the kingdom of God, the new creation, or Aslan's realm if you like. Life is fraught with challenges, heartbreaks, griefs, failures, disappointments, betrayal, and pain. It is there amid adversity, doubt, despair, fear, and tragedy that we look for strength from God. We continue to persist in the contest, to persevere in the race, and to press on toward the upward calling which is ours in Christ Jesus. Why? Because Scripture reminds us that God is for us, that Christ died and rose for us, and that the Holy Spirit is with us! This is why we can identify with John the Seer, in his exile on the island of Patmos, and see him as our "brother and companion in the suffering and kingdom and patient endurance that are ours in Jesus" (Revelation 1:9).

Moreover, the Spirit uses Scripture to mediate God's very own presence to us so that God's word provides us with the resilience that we need to keep going. The inspired Holy Scripture inspires us to get up, stand up, and not give up until we have attained the crown in which we will glory in the presence of the Lord Jesus himself. I find inspiration from the words of Psalm 77 about remembering the deeds of God in the past to give me hope and endurance in the present. I relish the words of Jesus in the Gospel about coming to him to find rest for my soul (Matthew 11:28) and

9. Walter Bauer, Frederick Danker, et al., *A Greek-English Lexicon of the New Testament and Other Early Christian Literature*, 3rd ed. (Chicago: University of Chicago Press, 2000), 1039.

remaining with him who alone has the words of eternal life (John 6:68). I find comfort meditating on Romans 8:31–39 about God's undefeatable and indefatigable love for us in Christ. I look ahead to a world with no more tears or terror as promised in Revelation 21–22. And most of all, I look to Jesus, who "for the joy set before him . . . endured the cross, scorning its shame, and sat down at the right hand of the throne of God" (Hebrews 12:2). I can endure all things because my Lord considered his suffering and humiliation for my redemption to be his joy!

We have the ability to endure because we have hope, or as Paul says, we have "endurance inspired by hope in our Lord Jesus Christ" (1 Thessalonians 1:3). Scripture narrates to us the substance and surety of our hope. Because of the testimony of Scripture, we have fled to God in order to take hold of the hope set before us in the gospel, and we are emboldened by it. Because of the hope laid out in Scripture, we can be confident in our faith and take risks for God because we know the hope that is offered to us. Because of the promises of Scripture, we have the hope of being seated with Christ as an anchor for the soul, firm and secure, rooted in the faithfulness of Jesus Christ, who reigns and intercedes for us at the Father's right hand. Scripture describes to us a hope in which nothing can separate us from the love of God; a hope that God will continue to deliver us in Christ and comfort our hearts by the Spirit. The reason we labor and strive in all things, spiritual and mundane, is that we have put our hope in the living God. This hope is not the pie-in-the-sky-when-you-die kind; it is hardly so cartoonish or fleeting. The substance of this hope, according to Scripture, is for us to dwell with Christ, to share in the new creation, and to participate in God's plan to put all things to rights.

Of course, for some people life is inherently hopeless, and any notion of hope is the worst of all possible mental diseases. The German philosopher Friedrich Nietzsche once sneered, "In reality, hope is the worst of all evils, because it prolongs man's torments."[10] Sadly, without hope we really do despair. Theologian Jürgen Moltmann said, "Living without hope is no longer living. Hell is hopelessness and it is not for nothing that at the entrance of Dante's hell there stand the words: 'Abandon hope, all ye who enter here.'"[11]

It is sad but true that without hope there is only despair and a futile attempt at survival. Without hope, we experience the paralysis of misery and succumb to the tyranny of cruel inevitability. Without hope, the best the secular world can do is pursue pleasure and power, try to minimize pain, or write psychedelic poetry. But because of the words of Jesus and the instruction of the apostles given to us in Scripture, we are not such a people. Yes, we all go through our own "slough of despond" and the "dark night of the soul"; but the light at the end of it is heaven's radiant glory, the never-failing, never-giving-up faithfulness of God, and surety of our reception into Christ's kingdom. We see the story of the gospel and the verdict of Scripture in N. T. Wright's poignant description: "Easter was when Hope in person surprised the whole world by coming forward from

---

10. Friedrich Nietzsche, *Human, All Too Human* (1878), #71.
11. Jürgen Moltmann, *Theology of Hope* (New York: Harper & Row, 1967), 32.

the future into the present."[12] We might even say that hope became flesh, dwelt among us, and now the word of hope goes forth into the whole world. It is thus no wonder that one of the most frequently repeated refrains in Psalm 119 is "I have put my hope in your word," because God's word is a word of promise and that promise *was* made good, *is* made good, and *will be* made good in Christ Jesus. Christianity is about the audacity of hope (hat tip to President Obama) because as J. I. Packer comments, "As God the Father is a God of hope, so his incarnate Son, Jesus of Nazareth, crucified, risen, reigning and returning, is a messenger, means and mediator of hope," for "the Bible is," he adds, "from Genesis to Revelation a book of hope."[13]

The hope envisioned in Scripture is not a blind faith or a cockeyed optimism. More properly, Christian hope as laid out in Scripture is the audacity of faith under adversity. Hope is the cheering in triumph for what others deem a lost cause. Hope denies that our lives don't matter. Hope is currency in the land of melancholy. Hope is the dancing when the music has long ceased. Hope is bread for the starved soul. Hope is the voice that whispers to us that "all things are possible." Hope is the grace to face our fears knowing that there is someone greater than the sum of all fears. Hope holds out a light rather than curses the dark. Hope is the physician of a terrified soul. Hope is the hero of the weak. Hope is defiance in the face of the tyrant. The gospel is the

---

12. N. T. Wright, *Surprised by Hope: Rethinking Heaven, the Resurrection, and the Mission of the Church* (San Francisco: HarperOne, 2009), 40–41.

13. J. I. Packer and Carolyn Nystrom, *Never beyond Hope: How God Touches and Uses Imperfect People* (Downers Grove, IL: InterVarsity Press, 2000), 13.

story of the invasion of hope into a world that knows only despair and darkness. The gospel tells us about men and women doomed for a hopeless end discovering in Christ Jesus an endless hope. Hope is that shameless confidence that Scripture's testimony to Jesus is totally trustworthy. As scholar Ernst Käsemann put it, "True theology . . . has to remain a pilgrim theology under the message of the gospel as a promise for the whole world—a theology of hope."[14]

LIVING IN THE LIGHT OF SCRIPTURE

Paul famously told Timothy that "all Scripture is God-breathed and is useful for teaching, rebuking, correcting and training in righteousness, so that the servant of God may be thoroughly equipped for every good work" (2 Timothy 3:16–17). That is a great starting point, worth memorizing, because Scripture keeps us on the straight and narrow. However, if we treat Scripture purely as a rule book or as a training manual, without understanding its saving story and without savouring its comforting promises, we will inevitably misuse it. Scripture is not a newspaper to whack you over the head with for being bad; more accurately, Scripture is a light in the darkness to guide your path and to illuminate your life with Christ. The purpose of Scripture is to give us knowledge of God, to nourish our faith, to drive us to love God and to love others, and to furnish us with the endurance that comes from Christian hope.

---

14. Ernst Käsemann, *Commentary on Romans* (Grand Rapids: Eerdmans, 1980), 242.

RECOMMENDED READING

Johnson, Luke Timothy. *Living the Gospel*. London: Continuum, 2005.

McKnight, Scot. *The Jesus Creed: Loving God, Loving Others*. Brewster, MA: Paraclete, 2019.

Packer, J. I. *Knowing God*. London: Hodder & Stoughton, 2013.

7

CHRIST IS THE CENTRE OF THE CHRISTIAN BIBLE

There are several books that whenever I see them in bookstores, in catalogues, or on someone's bookshelf I instinctively roll my eyes. Books that are either heretical, so cheesy you could dip your Doritos into them, or so self-serving that they come with a Botox voucher and selfie stick. But if there is one book that makes me mumble unsanctified thoughts, it would have to be Sally Lloyd-Jones's children's book *The Jesus Storybook Bible* and its subtitle *Every Story Whispers His Name.* Now, there is absolutely nothing wrong with this book; the concept is brilliant, the content is fine, the illustrations are wonderful, and the effect on readers is overwhelmingly positive. In fact, I read the book to my younger children at least once a year. So what is the source of my frustration? Well, simply this: I never wrote it! I wish I did write it because, given its sales success, I could be enjoying a nice early retirement with my wife in our love shack on the shores of Queensland's sunshine coast. But the primary reason I experience author envy is that this book has become the number one way that young evangelical parents are learning basic biblical theology and how to read the Bible with Jesus at the centre. I am serious! If it were not for *The Jesus Storybook Bible*, there would be a whole generation of evangelical men and women who have virtually no idea what the Old Testament is even about, how the Old Testament heads toward a certain climax, and how Jesus really is the goal of the biblical storyline. No wonder that every semester I usually meet a seminary student who confesses that it was thanks to reading *The Jesus Storybook Bible* to his or her children that they learned that Abraham came before Moses, that the Old Testament is not simply a random bunch of Sunday school tales but part of a single and unified story, and that Jesus is the climax of God's saving plan. And do not forget that the point of the book is true: every biblical story does whisper Jesus's name. Of course, while every story whispers "Jesus" (though not necessarily at the same volume or in the same key), the entirety of Scripture finds its coherence and unity in Jesus Christ. So Sally Lloyd-Jones gets a big high-five GIF from me on my Twitter account. She has made my job as a seminary professor so much easier by teaching parents, through reading to their children, some basics of the biblical story and its connection to Jesus.

WHAT IS BIBLICAL THEOLOGY?

Biblical theology can mean (a) looking at all of the theological themes in a single book; (b) mapping how a single theme like *covenant* or *kingdom* appears across both testaments; or (c) tracing the progress of the story, that is, redemptive history, across the testaments from Genesis to Revelation.

Lloyd-Jones tapped into an important conviction that Christians have about Scripture. The Christian church has ordinarily maintained that Jesus is indeed the interpretative centre of Scripture. That obviously holds true in the New Testament, but even the Old Testament should be understood in a Christ-centred fashion. The whole of Scripture either points ahead to Jesus as its fulfilment (Old Testament) or looks back to Jesus as the author and perfecter of our faith (New Testament). There is ample biblical material that makes this abundantly clear. What I want to do in this chapter is explain how. Precisely how is Jesus the centre of Scripture and how does the totality of Scripture find its unity and coherence in him?

"AND BEGINNING WITH MOSES"

According to Luke, it was the risen Jesus, speaking to two obtuse travelers on the road to Emmaus, who explained how the scriptural story climaxed with the Messiah's passion and resurrection: "How foolish you are, and how slow to believe all that the prophets have spoken! Did not the Messiah have to suffer these things and then enter his glory?" And Luke famously adds, "And beginning with Moses and all the Prophets, he explained to them what was said in all the Scriptures concerning himself" (Luke 24:25–27). In other words, Jesus himself was the first person who engaged in a Christocentric exposition of Scripture!

This is why I urge my seminary students to memorize a quotation from Paul's sermon in the synagogue at Pisidian Antioch about how all of God's promises find resolution in Jesus: "We tell you the good news: What God promised our ancestors he has fulfilled for us, their children, by raising up Jesus" (Acts 13:32–33). And Paul himself writes to the Corinthians: "For no matter how many promises God has made, they are 'Yes' in Christ" (2 Corinthians 1:20). **A central conviction in the Christian understanding of Scripture should be that Jesus fulfils what was promised to Israel about the Messiah in the Old Testament and Jesus remains the primary subject matter of the New Testament.**

I hope you are already convinced of this point: Jesus—his life, death, and resurrection, his status as Messiah and Lord, his identity as the Son of God—is the hermeneutical key to unlocking Scripture.

CHRISTOTELIC— CHRIST IS THE GOAL OF SCRIPTURE

How much Jesus is in your Old Testament? According to Ellen F. Davis, "Probably the most far-reaching issue separating traditional and modern (or postmodern) biblical interpretation is whether—and if so, how—to read the Old Testament as a witness to Jesus Christ."[1]

A Christian conviction is that the Old Testament is not merely the "Hebrew Bible" or the "Jewish Scriptures"; it is the first part of the Christian Bible completed by the New Testament. There is one God in three persons, one Bible with two testaments, and one story that climaxes in Jesus Christ. Old Testament scholar John Goldingay puts it well:

> Each individual biblical story belongs in the setting of the story as a whole, stretching from the Beginning to the End, with the Christ event at the center. The Second Testament story has to be read in light of the story related in the First and vice versa. The two Testaments are like the two acts of the one play. People cannot expect to understand Act II if they miss Act I, nor Act I if they leave at the intermission; neither act can be understood independently of the other.[2]

The upshot is that the Old Testament is not a dispensable prologue to Jesus, as it contains the first vital scenes

---

1. Ellen F. Davis, "Teaching the Bible Confessionally in the Church," in *The Art of Reading Scripture*, ed. E. F. Davis and R. B. Hays (Grand Rapids: Eerdmans, 2003), 18.

2. John E. Goldingay, *Models for Interpretation of Scripture* (Grand Rapids: Eerdmans, 1995), 62.

of the one story that climaxes in Jesus. The Old Testament is not merely a warm-up act to Jesus but is fully **christological** or, as Peter Enns calls it, **christotelic** in that Jesus is the goal and climax of God's revelation to Israel. By christotelic, I mean that Scripture is preparatory for and purposed for God's unveiling of himself in the man Jesus of Nazareth.[3]

The early church's christotelic reading of Scripture, i.e., the Old Testament, meant in practice reading Scripture from the vantage point of faith in Christ and studying Scripture with a Jesus lens. Jesus becomes present in the Old Testament, not based exclusively on literal readings nor purely reliant on a pattern of promise and fulfilment, but when viewed from the vantage point of gospel faith.[4] Identifying Jesus in the Old Testament in this fuller sense depends not solely on good exegesis but on a revelation (Luke 24:45), new birth (John 3:5–10), the Spirit's illumination (John 14:26; 15:26), and the removal of the veil of darkness (2 Corinthians 3:12–18). It is an interpretation driven by the experience of the risen Jesus, apostolic testimony, the wonder of worship, and the guidance of the Spirit. According to Peter Enns, "The apostles did not arrive at the conclusion that Jesus is Lord from a dispassionate, objective reading of the Old Testament.

---

3. On the Old Testament as "christotelic" see Peter Enns, *Inspiration and Incarnation: Evangelicals and the Problem of the Old Testament* (Grand Rapids: Baker, 2005), 152–60.

4. See Richard B. Hays, *Reading Backwards: A Figural Christology and the Fourfold Gospel Witness* (Waco, TX: Baylor University Press, 2014).

Rather, they began with what they knew to be true—the historical death and resurrection of the Son of God—and on the basis of that fact reread their Scripture in a fresh way."[5]

This explains why Christian interpreters believed that Old Testament saints had previously received the gospel in advance about Christ (Romans 10:16; Galatians 3:8; Hebrews 4:2; 1 Peter 3:19–20). This is why the Old Testament was regarded as a "shadow" of the realities that were realized in Christ (Colossians 2:17; Hebrews 8:5; 10:1). This explains why Matthew constantly emphasizes scriptural promises that have been fulfilled and patterns that have been rehearsed in Jesus (e.g., Matthew 2:14–18). This is why Jude believed that Jesus "at one time delivered his people out of Egypt" (Jude 5). This is why Paul could say that the rock that accompanied the Israelites in their wilderness wanderings and from which they drank was "Christ" (1 Corinthians 10:4); that God's promise for Abraham's "seed" pertains to none other than "Christ" (Galatians 3:16); that Adam was a "pattern of the one to come" (Romans 5:14); and that Christ is "the culmination of the law" (Romans 10:4).

Similarly, as we look at early church history, the same basic conviction that the Old Testament prefigures and prophesies Christ continues afresh. For example, Melito of Sardis (ca. AD 190) could write in his famous *Pascha* about how Christ appears in the Old Testament as a pattern,

---

5. Enns, *Inspiration and Incarnation*, 152.

an illustration, and an anticipation of the deliverance that
was yet to come:

> The Lord made advance preparation for his own
>   suffering in the patriarchs and in the prophets
>   and in the whole people; through the law and
>   the prophets he sealed them.
> That which more recently and most excellently
>   came to pass he arranged from of old.
> For when it would come to pass it would find
>   faith, having been foreseen of old.
>
> Thus the mystery of the Lord,
> prefigured from of old through the vision of a type,
> is today fulfilled and has found faith,
> even though people think it something new.
> For the mystery of the Lord is both new and old;
> old with respect to the law,
> but new with respect to grace.
> But if you scrutinize the type through its outcome
>   you will discern him.
>
> Thus if you wish to see the mystery of the Lord,
> look at Abel who is likewise slain,
> at Isaac who is likewise tied up,
> at Joseph who is likewise traded,
> at Moses who is likewise exposed,
> at David who is likewise hunted down,
> at the prophets who likewise suffer for the sake
>   of Christ.

> And look at the sheep, slaughtered in the land of
> Egypt, which saved Israel through its blood
> whilst Egypt was struck down.[6]

The apostles and church fathers did not read their Bible in a strictly literal manner nor indulge in endless allegory. But they did adopt a very consistent approach that saw the Old Testament as conveying a series of promises and patterns that found their fulfilment in Christ. They saw Christ in the Old Testament as the divine agent who was active in creation and in the exodus and was manifested in the angel of the Lord. They also found images of Christ all throughout the Law, Prophets, and Psalms.

This effort to find Jesus in the Old Testament is simply the logical outworking of the belief in God's faithfulness to Israel in the faithfulness of Jesus. If God sent forth Jesus Christ to bring salvation (Romans 8:3; Galatians 4:4–5; 1 John 4:9–10), then presumably he intimated this intention in the Holy Scriptures (Luke 24:44; Acts 13:33). If Jesus is God's ultimate agent of creation and redemption as the gospel claims, then presumably he has always had this role (John 1:1–2; Colossians 1:15; Hebrews 1:1–2). That is what motivated these early Christians to go to the Old Testament to search for him, to see him, and to find his presence in the Scriptures.

---

6. Melito of Sardis, *Pascha* 57–60 (Melito of Sardis, *On Pascha*, ed. and trans. Alistair C. Stewart [Yonkers, NY: St. Vladimir's Seminary Press, 2016], 67–68).

OKAY, BUT DON'T JESUSIFY EVERYTHING

Let's take a short intermission and make sure that our christotelic reading of Scripture does not get taken the wrong way. Yes, Jesus is the centre of Scripture, both the Old Testament and the New. Yes, reading the Old Testament through the eyes of faith requires, nay, necessitates that we believe that Moses, the Prophets, and the Psalms testify about Christ's person and work in a variety of ways. However, there are some other aspects to reading Scripture that we need to hold beside our christotelic reading strategy.

No Christomonism!

For a start, we must be wary of what we could call a **christomonistic** approach to Scripture. That is the problem whereby Scripture, especially the Old Testament, is preached almost exclusively as a way of intimating and exposing Christ, but then the actual content and concern of a specific passage are ignored (remember that stuff I told you in chapter 5 to pay attention to!). You probably know the problem I'm talking about—where the conclusion or application of every sermon is either "Isn't Jesus great!" or "Be more like Jesus!" Look, there are many appropriate times and places to do that sort of thing in preaching, to get your Jesus freak on; I'm down with that! However, not every time and place in Scripture is calling us to do that or to do that alone. Our reading of Scripture should not be one-dimensional or monolithic. The christotelic aspect of Scripture is important, even vital, but it is admittedly only one aspect of our reading strategy—we need to be attentive to more than just the christological testimony of Scripture.

For instance, one *could* preach the story of David and Bathsheba from 2 Samuel 11–12 and for application perhaps focus on how God was planning to send us a new king better than David, a greater David, a king who would not fail like David, and that king's name is Jesus. However, when I read the story of David and Bathsheba, I think we should say at least something about the dangers of adultery and covetousness, lust to the point of violence, male power and female exploitation, and the consequences of people's actions. Also, in preaching the parable of the prodigal son in Luke 15:11–32, I'd want to say more than Jesus brings prodigal sons and daughters home to God. I'd want to say something about God's gracious and compassionate fatherhood and warn against being the sneering older brother. In other words, a christotelic approach to Scripture is something we have in addition to, not as an alternative to, the theological, ethical, and churchly dimensions of Scripture. Yes, "every story whispers his name," but Jesus's name is not the only name in every story, not the only part in every story, not the only subplot in every story, and not the only point of every story. So don't reject christotelic readings as allegory, but don't be a christomonistic reader either. Don't be someone who so searches for Jesus in portions of Scripture that they ignore the various plots, themes, lessons, and layers of scriptural meaning.

Without forfeiting the christotelic horizon of Scripture, we need to pay attention to other dimensions of Scripture pertaining to God, ethics, and the church.

Theocentric Dimension

Besides our christotelic interpretation, we need to be **theocentric**. By theocentric, I mean that we recognize that Scripture is a God story! This is a fairly uncontroversial assumption that requires us to pay attention to how God is a central character in the biblical story. As such, we need to detect God's providence behind every scene; notice instances of God's love; explore God's relationship with the patriarchs, Israel, prophets, and kings; pay heed to God's demands on his people; and give attention to God's redemptive work for his people. And when I say "God," I don't mean the benign cosmic Santa Claus of cultural Christianity; no, I mean the Trinity—a thick and fulsome account of the Christian deity as a tripersonal being. We read Scripture attentive to the triune God, one God in three persons—Father, Son, and Holy Spirit—who exist in one substance, power, and eternity. Scripture illuminates the Trinity and is illuminated by the Trinity.

The scriptural story involves God the Father, God the Son, and God the Holy Spirit. Every moment in the story tells us something of God's character, God's purposes, God's worship, God's demands, and God's love. That reaches a climax in the sending of Jesus, a sending that is intimated in the Old Testament, and its meaning is actualized in our hearts by the Holy Spirit. The theocentric perspective of Scripture means it is about God as one who creates, commands, calls, covenants, and consummates all things. The Bible could not be a Jesus book unless it were first a God book inspired and illuminated by the Holy Spirit.

Moral Dimension

Christian Scripture possesses an important **moral dimension**.[7] Scripture is one of the chief instruments by which God shapes our character, forms our conscience, chastens our sin, and conforms us to the teachings and example of Jesus. Yes, I know this can easily descend into moralism or even legalism, reducing Scripture to a list of divinely sanctioned rules. But Scripture really does set before us a moral vision, patterns to emulate, and commands to obey. The scriptural narrative shapes people according to the character of God, to keep the pattern of Christ, and to bear the fruit of the Holy Spirit. Scripture imposes on us a story, and it is this story that shapes our actions just as much as it should determine our beliefs. Do not, then, neglect the ethical horizon of Scripture lest you end up becoming morally vacuous.

Reading the Bible for ethical formation and reading the Bible in a christotelic way are not mutually exclusive. According to African theologian Samuel Waje Kunhiyop:

People are not Christians merely because they believe in God or some supernatural power; they are Christians because they believe that Jesus is the Son of God who died and rose from the grave and gives every believer the power to live a moral life. As the Son of God, Jesus is the most complete revelation

7. See Jason Hood, "Christ-Centred Interpretation Only? Moral Instruction from Scripture's Self-Interpretation as Caveat and Guide," *Scottish Bulletin of Evangelical Theology* 27 (2009): 50–69.

of who God is. He is thus our ethical paradigm, in other words, our example of how we should live. . . . Following in Christ's steps means demonstrating the same qualities that Jesus demonstrated in his earthly life. Paul regularly draws out the implications of Jesus' death and resurrection for our ethical conduct (Rom 6:1–14; 8:17, 29–30; 15:1–7; 1 Cor 10:2–11; 2 Cor 4:7–15; 12:9–10; Gal 2:19–20; 5:24; 6:14).[8]

Church Dimension

Finally, Scripture should be read **ecclesiocentrically** (*ecclesia* comes from the Greek work *ekklēsia*, for "church" or "assembly"). Scripture is in a sense also about the church. Paul makes an interesting point when telling the Corinthians that the things written in Scripture were written for their instruction since they are the ones "upon whom the end of the ages has come" (1 Corinthians 10:11 [RSV]). That is not to put the church, ourselves so to speak, at the centre of God's purpose and plans. Even so, we need to remember that God's redemptive power has invaded the present age, exploded upon the church, and waits for a future fulfilment. God's plan is for God's people to reign with Christ in a new creation, in a new heaven and a new earth, experiencing the climactic and joyous union of God with his people. As such, God really wants us to become little miniatures of his Son, little icons of Christ, to inhabit

---

8. Samuel Waje Kunhiyop, *African Christian Ethics* (Nairobi: Hippo, 2008), 54.

his new world, to experience the promise of never-ending peace and everlasting life, to enjoy him forever, and to participate in Christ's cosmic lordship. The church is no mere passive collection of religious consumers waiting to be wafted up to heaven on a moment's notice. Much to the contrary, the people of God are the creaturely means through whom God's witness and word are carried forward into the world, until the day when God fills all things in every way, until the moment when the kingdoms of the nations are displaced by the kingdom of our God and his Messiah. In the interim, however, the church is now an ambassador of God's reign, and in the future we are destined to be co-regents with Christ. Hence, in the final vision of John of Patmos's revelation, we read: "They will not need the light of a lamp or the light of the sun, for the Lord God will give them light. And they will reign for ever and ever" (Revelation 22:5). If this is all true, and I firmly believe it is, then we must read Scripture much like Paul told the Corinthians to, with an eye to how Scripture instructs the church, and with a mind for how God's purposes culminate in the union of Christ and his church, ever aware that Scripture points to the role that the church plays in the unfolding revelation of God's mysterious purposes.

SHOULD WE INTERPRET THE SCRIPTURES LIKE THE APOSTLES DID?

One cheeky thing I do with my students is take them through some New Testament passages to see how the Old

Testament is being interpreted by the apostles. I get them to read the infancy narratives of Matthew 1–2, the Johannine passion narrative in John 19, Paul's lengthy discourse about Israel in Romans 9–11, Paul's polemical argumentation in Galatians 3–4, and John's vision of the woman and the dragon in Revelation 11–12. I then ask them, "Should we interpret the Old Testament like the early church did?" These chapters contain some genuinely perplexing examples of how the apostles, evangelists, and early church in general interpreted the Old Testament. I mean, Paul mentions taking things "allegorically" (Galatians 4:24 NRSV); John the Seer says his vision should be understood "spiritually" (Revelation 11:8 CEB); many of Matthew's Old Testament citations do not strike you as obvious messianic texts when read on their own terms; and Paul's argumentation about Israel is densely packed with an avalanche of citations and allusions to the Old Testament to the point of being overwhelmed by them. It is no wonder that many of my students feel conflicted, confused, and apprehensive, and that many are reluctant to follow the apostles in their biblical interpretation.

Now this is an allegory: these women are two covenants. One woman, in fact, is Hagar, from Mount Sinai, bearing children for slavery. Now Hagar is Mount Sinai in Arabia and corresponds to the present Jerusalem, for she is in slavery with her children. But the other woman corresponds to the Jerusalem above; she is free, and she is our mother. For it is written,

"Rejoice, you childless one, you who bear no children,
     burst into song and shout, you who endure no
          birth pangs;
for the children of the desolate woman are more
     numerous
     than the children of the one who is married."
     (Galatians 4:24–27 NRSV)

Their dead bodies will lie on the street of the great city that is *spiritually* called Sodom and Egypt, where also their Lord was crucified. And for three and a half days, members of the peoples, tribes, languages, and nations will look at their dead bodies, but they won't let their dead bodies be put in a tomb. (Revelation 11:8–9 CEB)

The early church's interpretation of the Old Testament appears foreign to how most Christians have been taught to read Scripture. Some suppose that the apostles are able to undertake their intricate interpretative maneuvers with christological cartwheels because they have a special license to do some crazy things. As a result, we should obey them, but we should not follow them in their interpretive methods. However, in my defense of apostolic biblical interpretation, I tell my students this: *if* Jesus is the climax of the covenant, *if* Jesus is the fulfilment of the law, *if* Jesus is the one whom the prophets were pointing ahead to, *if* the Scriptures indeed testify to Jesus, *if* the Old Testament is filled with types that anticipate Jesus as Lord and Saviour, *then* it is not merely legitimate to read Scripture in a christotelic fashion, but it is demanded as an article of faith. To read Scripture as a Christian is to regard Scripture as finding its substance, coherence, and unity in Jesus Christ. As Christians whose faith was established on the foundations of the prophets and the apostles (Ephesians 2:20), we are obligated to follow after their strategy for preaching and teaching Scripture. So, yes, you should interpret the Bible like the apostles did if you claim to belong to a church that is based on the gospel that the apostles preached. What is more, after two thousand years of interpretation, this apostolic manner of Christian reading, with its spiritual dimension and christotelic focus, is far more stable, enduring, and coherent than the endless fads and fragmentation that have characterized secular approaches to the Bible.

THE WHOLE COUNSEL OF GOD WITH WISE INTERPRETATION

Paul told the Ephesians that in his ministry he had not refrained from declaring to them "the whole counsel of God" (Acts 20:27 ESV). By which Paul means he did not hesitate to set out God's will as found in the entirety of the Scriptures. What I've tried to explain in this chapter is that learning the whole counsel of God requires a holistic and wise interpretive approach. Here is the takeaway: Scripture is christotelic—Jesus is the goal and unity of Scripture. In fact, we know that because Jesus himself interpreted Scripture as a testimony to himself. However, don't get christomonistic about it, and make sure that you pay attention to the theocentric, moral, and ecclesial aspects of Scripture too. In addition to that, looking at how the apostles interpreted the Old Testament is one of the best starting points to begin interpreting the New Testament in christotelic fashion. Our approach to Scripture should stand in continuity with the apostles if we claim to be part of an assembly that traces its lineage back to the apostles and if we regard ourselves as custodians of the gospel that the apostles themselves proclaimed. To be brutally honest, you should do that all the more if you are a Protestant because this was partly the reason for the Reformation: retrieving the apostolic gospel and the apostolic way of reading Scripture! So keep close to the apostles as they try to keep close to Jesus in Scripture, ever mindful of the theological, moral, and ecclesial dimensions of Scripture.

RECOMMENDED READING

Davis, Ellen F. *Wondrous Depth: Preaching the Old Testament*. Louisville: Westminster John Knox, 2005.

Greidanus, Sidney. *Preaching Christ from the Old Testament*. Grand Rapids: Eerdmans, 1999.

Smith, Brandon, and Everett Berry. *They Spoke of Me: How Jesus Unlocks the Old Testament*. Spring Hill, TN: Rainer, 2018.

Williams, Michael. *How to Read the Bible through a Jesus Lens: A Guide to Christ-Focused Reading of Scripture*. Grand Rapids: Zondervan, 2012.

Wright, Christopher J. H. *Knowing Jesus through the Old Testament*. Downers Grove, IL: InterVarsity Press, 1992.

THE TOP FIVE OLD TESTAMENT TEXTS IN THE NEW TESTAMENT

One interesting facet of apostolic preaching is that the apostles repeatedly claimed that the gospel's narration about the Messiah's death, resurrection, and exaltation happened "according to Scripture" or in "fulfilment" of Scripture (e.g., John 2:22; Acts 13:33; 1 Corinthians 15:3–4). However, which precise Scriptures did the apostles and first Christians have in mind? Which scriptural stories and types were they recalling? Where in the Old Testament did they look for prophetic proof of their message?

For me as a biblical-studies professor, one of the most personally traumatizing moments in my teaching experience, and a cause for constant worry about the state of biblical education in our churches, is when I ask a new cohort of students, "How would you preach the gospel from the Old Testament?" Hey, anyone can preach the gospel from Romans, Acts, or the Gospel of Matthew, but what about from the Old Testament? Remember, the apostles did not write the New Testament ten minutes after Pentecost, so which Old Testament Scriptures did they preach from when they preached Jesus as Lord and Messiah? When I ask that question to first-year seminary students, supposedly from good Bible-believing churches, I get dumbfounded facial expressions, kind of like deer with hipster beards and chinos in headlights, or students throwing up their hands and appealing to Psalm 23 off the top of their head! Ironically enough, despite the popularity of Psalm 23 in personal piety, Psalm 23 is never once quoted in the New Testament. So I tell them to try harder, and all I get in response is zip and zilch.

Below, I provide the top five Old Testament texts that appear in the New Testament, with an explanation of what made them so conducive to apostolic teaching and useful in evangelistic preaching.

PSALM 118:22–26

The stone the builders rejected
    has become the cornerstone;
the Lord has done this,
    and it is marvelous in our eyes.
The Lord has done it this very day;
    let us rejoice today and be glad.

Lord, save us!
    Lord, grant us success!

> Blessed is he who comes in the name of the Lord.
> From the house of the Lord we bless you.

When Elizabeth I, daughter of the English king Henry VIII, found out that she was going to become queen, she allegedly fell to the ground and cited Psalm 118:22 in Latin. Her joy and astonishment was that, instead of being executed by her sister Queen Mary as a Protestant heretic and a rival to her throne, Elizabeth was now to become queen after Mary's impending death. It was the ultimate reversal for Elizabeth: from potential martyrdom to actual monarchy! Similarly, Psalm 118, understood in its original context, is a thanksgiving psalm that celebrates God's reversal of fortunes for the Hebrews when they were delivered from Egypt, and thereafter pilgrims would sing it on entering Jerusalem for Passover or even during the Passover celebration itself.

In the New Testament, Jesus quotes this psalm after telling the parable of the wicked tenants. The idea was that he and his followers were the ones to be rejected by the Judean leadership ("the stone the builders rejected"), and yet they would be vindicated by God and would be the recipients of God's kingdom and constitute the "cornerstone" of the renewed Israel (Matthew 21:42–44). According to Luke, Peter delivered a speech to the Jerusalem elders and priestly rulers, in which he told them: "Jesus is 'the stone you builders rejected, which has become the cornerstone.' Salvation is found in no one else, for there is no other name under heaven given to mankind by which we must be saved" (Acts 4:11–12). Peter, in his own letter to the churches of northern Asia Minor, combines Isaiah 28:16 about a precious and chosen stone laid in Zion with Psalm 118 about the rejected cornerstone. The result is that, just like Jesus, the churches are rejected and yet chosen by God to be his spiritual house and spiritual people: "As you come to him, the living Stone—rejected by humans but chosen by God and precious to him—you also, like living stones, are being built into a spiritual house to be a holy priesthood, offering spiritual sacrifices acceptable to God through Jesus Christ" (1 Peter 2:4–5). Jesus might have been rejected by the Judean leaders and crucified by the Romans, and the message about him mocked by Greek philosophers, but what matters is what God has declared about him and his people: he is the chosen cornerstone upon which Israel's God has created a renewed Israel consisting of Jews and gentiles united by faith in him.

LEVITICUS 19:18

"Love your neighbor as yourself."

In the popular British science fiction show *Doctor Who*, some crazy old lady announces that the KJV Old Testament states, "Thou shalt not suffer a witch to live," to which the doctor replies that the sequel to the Old Testament—the New Testament—says, "Love thy neighbour." Sadly, the good doctor might need to take Bible 101. Yes, the New Testament does indeed say, "Love thy neighbour," but it does so by quoting Leviticus 19:18 from the Old Testament! So you can't play the mean and loveless commands of the Old Testament off against the love and mercy of the New Testament. If Christianity has one distinctive approach to its ethics, it would have to be the priority of love for relationships not only with fellow Christians but even with those who are outside the church.[1]

---

1. The love command is also found in Jewish literature and analogous

Christians are defined by love for God and love for neighbour. And that ethos is firmly rooted in the Old Testament: it derives from God's revelation of himself to Israel, and love is intrinsic to the ethics and ethos of Israel's religious life. The love command of Leviticus 19:18, given to mitigate the possibility of a person seeking vengeance against a fellow Israelite, was taken up by Jesus, incorporated into his teaching, and came to constitute a distinctive feature of his instructions to his followers. According to Jesus, kingdom people love their neighbours, even their enemies and persecutors, and this is the summation of the entire Torah (Matthew 5:43; 22:39). Interesting too is that both Paul (Romans 13:9–10; Galatians 5:14) and James (James 2:8) rehearse the notion of the love command as the summation of the Torah and consider the love command to be the single most important aspect of Christian behavior. Quite naturally, the love command and the discipline of love-in-practice became a distinctive feature of Christian spirituality, social ethics, and communal life.

PSALM 110:1, 4

The LORD says to my lord:

"Sit at my right hand
until I make your enemies
a footstool for your feet.". . .

---

examples abound in Greco-Roman writings too. Roughly contemporary with Paul, the philosopher Epictetus urged that a philosopher who is flogged "must love the ones who flog him as if he were their father or brother" (Arrian, *Epict. Diss.* 3.22.54). Almost a century after Jesus, Rabbi Akiba could call the Levitical love command "the greatest principle in the law" (*Sipra Lev* §200).

> The Lord has sworn
>> and will not change his mind:
> "You are a priest forever,
>> in the order of Melchizedek."

I recently saw the smash-hit musical *Hamilton*, which is replete with Christian themes and so much fun to watch. In one song, the narrator, Aaron Burr, describes Alexander Hamilton's appointment as General George Washington's chief of staff as Hamilton being "seated at the right hand of the father," and those words are a direct quote from the Apostles' Creed, which itself is a summary of Psalm 110:1 and its many allusions in the New Testament.

Psalm 110 is the most frequently cited, alluded to, and echoed Old Testament passage in the entire New Testament. It is everywhere! Now, in its original context, Psalm 110 is a royal psalm about the triumph of the Davidic dynasty over the surrounding pagan kingdoms. A courtier pronounces how "the Lord" (*Yahweh*) promises to "my lord" (*Adonai*, i.e., the Davidic king) to subjugate his enemies. However, Jesus and the early church understood David to be the speaker of the psalm whereby the Lord (*Yahweh*) promised David's Lord (the Messiah) to subjugate his enemies. This is why Jesus asked the Pharisees how the Messiah could be David's son since David himself calls the Messiah "Lord." The implication being that while the Messiah might be a son of David, he is more than a son of David—he is preexistent and destined to share in the sphere of divine sovereignty (Matthew 22:41–46).

Other New Testament authors reflected on Psalm 110 in relation to Jesus and believed that God "seated him at his right hand in the heavenly realms, far above all rule and authority, power and dominion" (Ephesians 1:20–21); Jesus "sat down at the right hand of the Majesty in heaven" (Hebrews 1:3); and Jesus "has gone into heaven and is at God's right hand—with angels, authorities and powers in submission to him" (1 Peter 3:22). Jesus's exaltation to the seat of divine power is accentuated in Revelation 4–5. There we encounter a vision report about the heavenly throne room of God and the worship therein, but it is soon clear that the Lamb of God shares God's throne, stands at the centre of the throne, and receives the same chorus of heavenly worship as God the Father. In other words, when Psalm 110 is viewed christologically, Jesus is not merely chilling out in heaven; rather, in his glorified human body, he is currently executing divine regency over the affairs of the universe.

DANIEL 7:13

In my vision at night I looked, and there before me was one like a son of man, coming with the clouds of heaven. He approached the Ancient of Days and was led into his presence.

The Jewish historian Josephus, writing in the aftermath of the Jewish revolt against Rome and the destruction of the temple in AD 66–70, referred to an "ambiguous oracle" that portrayed a figure, a charismatic or military leader, who would subdue the Romans and conquer the inhabitable earth. I, and many others, think that Josephus was referring to the book of Daniel, especially chapters 2, 7, and 9, when he mentioned this oracle.[2] Daniel is a complex document for all sorts of reasons—language, date,

---

2. See Josephus, *War* 6.312–15; 4.388, and discussion in N. T. Wright, *The New Testament and the People of God* (London: SPCK, 1992), 314.

setting, authorship, etc. However, it is clear that Daniel 7, with its vision of the four beasts and the Son of Man who is enthroned before the Ancient of Days, was a very significant text for the early church. Disagree with me if you like, but I think the four beasts represent the Babylonian, Persian, Macedonian, and Seleucid empires, and the arrogant horn is probably Antiochus Epiphanes IV, the Syrian king who desecrated the Jerusalem temple in 167 BC, and who thereafter became the prototype of all anti-God and antichrist figures in Jewish and Christian traditions.

These beasts are the pagan powers of the world that stand against God and his people, and the looming question is whether God will stand for it. The answer to that question is given in the narrative immediately after the description of the four beasts and the emergence of the arrogant horn, in which we have a mysterious throne scene where "one like a son of man" comes before the Ancient of Days and is led into his presence, and we are told: "He was given authority, glory and sovereign power; all nations and peoples of every language worshiped him. His dominion is an everlasting dominion that will not pass away, and his kingdom is one that will never be destroyed" (Daniel 7:14). In my mind, the "one like a son of man" refers to God's messianic king, God's kingdom, and God's people (Daniel 7:18, 27). Daniel's vision of a human figure enthroned with God, symbolizing Israel's triumph over the pagan empires and their pantheon of gods, was taken up in Jewish and Christian literature and became a staple of messianic expectations and hopes for the future deliverance of the Jewish nation.

The title "Son of Man" is disputed: Does it merely mean "son of Adam" or "human being"? Is it an Aramaic idiom for "I" or "someone in my position"? Is it indebted to Daniel 7, and if so, precisely how? The Gospels use the title as Jesus's preferred means of self-designation, most probably as a cryptic allusion to the mystery that surrounds his role in God's kingdom as its Messiah and inaugurator.[3] If you examine Mark 13, the Olivet Discourse, you may detect how Daniel 7 has shaped much of the language about the Son of Man's future coming to bring judgment on the Jerusalem temple and to save the elect from the Roman siege of Jerusalem. It is also interesting that at Jesus's trial before the Sanhedrin, Jesus replied to a messianic question from the high priest Caiaphas with a claim that he, as the Son of Man, will be enthroned at the right hand of God. Jesus's words deliberately and provocatively conflate language from Psalm 110:1 and Daniel 7:13, which prompts an accusation of blasphemy against Jesus by the high priest (Matthew 26:64–65; Mark 14:62–64; Luke 22:67–70). The imagery here implies that Jesus will—and already does—share in God's very own lordship.[4] Although the title "Son of Man" is scarcely used outside of the Gospels (Acts 7:56; Hebrews 2:6; Revelation 1:13; 14:14), in the early church's memory, it seems to have described Jesus as *the* human figure who would be enthroned before God and bring deliverance to God's people.

PSALM 2:7

> He said to me, "You are my son;
>> today I have become your father."

It has been a while since the British have had a coronation ceremony to appoint a new monarch. Queen Elizabeth II has reigned

---

3. See Michael F. Bird, *Are You the One Who Is to Come? The Historical Jesus and the Messianic Question* (Grand Rapids: Baker, 2009), 77–116.

4. Joel Marcus, "Mark 14:61: 'Are You the Messiah—Son of God?,'" *Novum Testamentum* 31 (1989): 139 (125–41).

since 1953, and Prince Charles will probably have to wait a few more years yet for his coronation service as king. In Psalm 2, we have a coronation psalm, a text that celebrates God commissioning a new Israelite king as his "son" and so fulfilling the promises that God made to David about his descendants, "When your days are over and you rest with your ancestors, I will raise up your offspring to succeed you, your own flesh and blood, and I will establish his kingdom. He is the one who will build a house for my Name, and I will establish the throne of his kingdom forever. I will be his father, and he will be my son" (2 Samuel 7:12–14). Early Christian authors thought that Psalm 2:7 was appropriate to describe Jesus as one commissioned to be the messianic king and Suffering Servant at his baptism (Mark 1:11) and one installed by God at his resurrection as the exalted Son who reigns with Israel's God (Acts 13:33; Hebrews 1:5; 5:5). Looking at the rest of the psalm, God has appointed Jesus Christ, the Son of God, to rule the nations and to subdue the kings of the nations with an iron scepter (Psalm 2:9; Acts 4:24–28; Revelation 2:27; 12:5; 19:15). The early church looked at Jesus, looked at Psalm 2, looked at Jesus again, and concluded: now, this is God's Son, this is God's king, this is the one who is going to rule over the nations.

We could discuss so many other Old Testament texts and how they appear in the New Testament, in particular, the fourth Servant Song of Isaiah 52–53, parts of Jeremiah and Zechariah, stories from Genesis and Exodus, elements of Proverbs, and more. Suffice to say for now, the early church read their Jewish Scriptures through a Christ-lens that made Jesus the centrepiece and organic unity of the totality of Scripture.

SCRIPTURE INDEX

SUBJECT INDEX

What Christians Ought to Believe

An Introduction to Christian Doctrine through the Apostles' Creed

Michael F. Bird

In *What Christians Ought to Believe*, Michael Bird opens our eyes to the possibilities of the Apostles' Creed as a way to explore and understand the basic teachings of the Christian faith.

Bringing together theological commentary, tips for application, and memorable illustrations, *What Christians Ought to Believe* summarizes the basic tenets of the Christian faith, using the Apostles' Creed as its entryway. After first emphasizing the importance of creeds for the formation of the Christian faith, each chapter, following the Creed's outline, introduces the Father, the Son, the Spirit, the church, and the life to come.

What Christians Ought to Believe Video Lectures

An Introduction to Christian Doctrine through the Apostles' Creed

Michael F. Bird

What Christians Ought to Believe Video Lectures, featuring author and professor Michael Bird, is a full video introduction to Christian doctrine that uses the Apostles' Creed as the entryway to show what Christians should believe about God, Jesus, the Spirit, the church, and the life to come.

Evangelical Theology, Second Edition

A Biblical and Systematic Introduction

Michael F. Bird

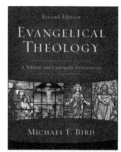

Gospel-Centered Theology for Today

Evangelical Theology, Second Edition helps today's readers understand and practice the doctrines of the Christian faith by presenting a gospel-centered theology that is accessible, rigorous, and balanced. According to author Michael Bird, the gospel is the fulcrum of Christian doctrine; the gospel is where God meets us and where we introduce the world to God. As such, an authentically evangelical theology is the working out of the gospel in the various doctrines of Christian theology.

Evangelical Theology Video Lectures

A Biblical and Systematic Introduction

Michael F. Bird

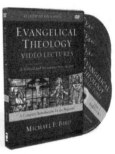

Evangelical Theology Video Lectures presents a gospel-centered theology that is accessible and balanced. The gospel is the fulcrum of Christian doctrine. As such, an authentically evangelical theology is the working out of the gospel in the various doctrines of theology that should shape how we think, pray, preach, teach, and minister.

The New Testament in Its World

An Introduction to the History, Literature, and Theology of the First Christians

N. T. Wright and Michael F. Bird

The New Testament in Its World by N. T. Wright and Michael F. Bird is the definitive introduction to the New Testament, presenting the New Testament books as a literary, narrative, and social phenomena located in the world of Second Temple Judaism and early Christianity.

The New Testament in Its World Video Lectures

An Introduction to the History, Literature, and Theology of the First Christians

N. T. Wright and Michael F. Bird

At over thirteen hours of content, these lectures are the definitive video introduction to the history, literature, and theology of the New Testament. Numerous bonus lectures are also included.